Astonishing Survival Stories from Around the World

Incredible Accounts that Inspire Indomitable Spirit

Phoenix MacLeod

CONTENTS

Introduction   1

1. Survival in the Sahara   5

2. Endurance in Antarctica   17

3. Resilience in Japanese Jungles   33

4. Two-mile Fall from the Peruvian Sky   45

5. Odyssey in the Ocean   55

6. Triumph in the Andes   69

7. 438 Days Adrift in the Pacific   79

8. 200-foot Plunge off a California Cliff   89

9. Teamwork in Tham Luang Cave   95

Conclusion   113

Please Help Other Readers   124

Free PDF Booklet for You   125

References   127

I

SURVIVAL IN THE SAHARA

Northwest Coast of the Sahara Desert, 1815

The world of the early 1800s was vastly different than it is today. Today, we have the luxury of flying supplies and goods via airplanes worldwide in a matter of hours. In the early 1800s, goods and supplies were sent on long voyages via seafaring ships, thousands of which crisscrossed the world's oceans simultaneously. These voyages took several months to complete and were fraught with danger, including major sea storms and hostile forces in faraway lands.

James Riley was captain of one of these trading ships, the appropriately named Commerce, *in service of the United States Merchant Navy. In August 1815, Riley was commanding the ship around the coast of Africa en route back to America with a full load of exotic goods. Little did Riley know at the time that he and his crew would soon become embroiled in the biggest battle for survival of their entire lives.*

We know what happened because Riley recounted the events in his 1817 memoir Sufferings in Africa. *What follows is a summary of how Riley and his crew told it.*

CAPTAIN RILEY LIVED IN a time when the Age of Exploration was coming to an end. The Age of Exploration is considered to have begun in the late 15th century, and it played a crucial role in shaping the course of history and impacting global trade. By the early 1800s, much of the world had been explored from the initial exploratory voyages, but the routes that were discovered from these voyages continued to influence shipping practices, particularly concerning the transport of goods to and from the United States. At this time, of course, the United States was a nation still in its infancy, struggling to carve out a place for itself on the world stage.

During the Age of Exploration, European powers sought new trade routes to Asia and around Africa, leading to the discovery of the Americas. This era saw the rise of transoceanic trade routes, connecting the Old World to the New. By the early 1800s, these trade routes had become so well-established that they were crisscrossed hundreds, if not thousands, of times by military and civilian vessels alike. These routes also served to connect America with the rest of the outside world, and without them, America would have been largely cut off and incapable of making trade with Old World nations.

As a burgeoning economic power, the United States relied heavily on shipping to transport goods to and from its shores and to keep its economy growing. Exports from the country included agricultural products such as cotton, tobacco, and grain, as well as timber and raw materials. These goods were transported to Europe and other markets.

Conversely, the United States imported manufactured goods, textiles, and luxury items from Europe and other trading partners. Reliance on shipping as a primary means of transportation was integral to the country's economic development during this era. Coastal ports such as New York, Boston, and New Orleans emerged as vital hubs for trade and commerce.

Riley's ship was just one of many that transported goods to help the young United States grow. However, Riley and his men were about to find themselves up against the Sahara Desert—the largest hot desert in the world, which spans all the way across North Africa and covers vast expanses of land stretching over 3.6 million square miles.

The Sahara is known for its extreme aridity and scorching temperatures. The desert's climate is characterized by high daytime temperatures exceeding 122 degrees Fahrenheit and significant temperature fluctuations between day and night. The Sahara receives minimal precipitation, with large areas experiencing less than an inch of rainfall annually, making it one of the driest regions on Earth.

The towering dunes can reach heights of over 500 feet and continuously shift and reshape due to the persistent winds that sweep across the desert.

As a result, navigating across them is very difficult, and walking up and down them can be very exhausting.

There are few places as desolate on Earth as the Sahara.

———— ✦ ————

JAMES RILEY WAS BORN in Middletown, Connecticut, in 1777, as the Revolutionary War broke out. He was an American sea captain and adventurer. Before the shipwreck that would define his legacy, Riley led a life deeply intertwined with the maritime world of the early 19th century.

His seafaring career began at a young age, and he rose through the ranks, earning a well-deserved reputation as a capable and seasoned sailor. His skills and experiences eventually led him to the position of captain.

In Riley's time, maritime trade was a vital component of global commerce, and captains like him played a crucial role in facilitating trade routes between nations. Riley engaged in this dynamic industry by commanding merchant vessels involved in trade between the United States and other parts of the world.

In the summer of 1815, James Riley assumed command of *Commerce*, built for transatlantic trade for the United States government. Riley's assignment was to conduct a trading mission to collect exotic goods along the rugged coast of Africa that could then be brought back to America.

The voyage went largely according to plan until the return phase. Once loaded with goods, Riley directed Commerce around the southern tip of Africa and up along the western African coastline. As the ship crossed the Atlantic to return to the East Coast of the United States, it encountered the tempestuous wrath of the very unpredictable ocean.

Commerce could not continue, so Riley turned the ship around to return to Africa. The vessel was battered and worn from the storms, and while it was still afloat, Riley knew it needed repairs before they could make another attempt across the open sea.

Riley and the crew anchored *Commerce* off the northwest African coast of the Sahara Desert. The coastline was arid and desolate, and Riley feared they would not find the natural resources to make the necessary repairs to the ship.

It was while Riley and a few crew members came to shore to search for resources that things went awry.

An Arab tribesman armed with a spear appeared on the horizon. Uninvited, he walked down to where Riley and the crew had parked their rowboat and began to take their supplies from the boat. Riley could tell the tribesman was unintimidated by their presence, so he directed his crew to safety while he engaged the tribesman in conversation.

The tribesman, however, left and then returned with reinforcements consisting of more armed tribesmen. Riley quickly discerned that their lives were in danger and again engaged them verbally to negotiate for their lives. He convinced the tribesman to spare their lives in exchange for money.

Riley, however, had no intention of giving the tribesmen anything.

After calling for another crew member to come ashore with the agreed payment, Riley seized his opportunity. In a daring sprint, he went for the launch boat to make his escape, but the crew member who had come ashore was not so fortunate and met his tragic fate at the hands of the armed tribesmen.

With their lives hanging in the balance, Riley and his surviving crew navigated their badly damaged ship southward along the African coast, desperately seeking resources for the repairs the vessel needed. Their voyage led them about 200 miles until they found solace on a beach backed by towering cliffs.

To the crew's disappointment, however, they still couldn't find the necessary resources to repair the ship. By this point, *Commerce* was in such bad condition that it couldn't go any further.

After making landfall on the beach, Riley ascended one of the cliffs to see what was on the other side, desperately seeking signs of water (which was running low) and other needed resources. But at the summit, the vastness of the world's largest desert sprawled before him. Instead of the freshwater and wooded oasis he sought, Riley faced the daunting expanse of the Sahara.

Riley returned to his men and shared the harsh truth: they had reached the outskirts of the Sahara, where daytime temperatures soared to extremes of 130 degrees Fahrenheit and plummeted nearly 100 degrees to freezing temperatures after nightfall.

The men were now confronted with a stark reality. With the open sea behind them and the scorching Sahara Desert ahead, they only had one choice: take their chances in the desert or die by the shoreline. Fueled by the hope that they could find the resources they needed to make repairs and, in the process, locate a source of food and water, they embarked inland into the desert.

THE SAHARA PROVED TO be even worse than they had expected. As the days passed, Riley and his men, fatigued and demoralized, faced the seeming inevitability of their fate. They ran out of food and water and were unable to find more. Extreme hunger and thirst set in, and coupled with the freezing temperatures at night and the overbearing sun during the day, the men were pushed to the brink. The men could not get much sleep due to the frigid temperatures, and their progress during the day was slow under the unrelenting heat.

Within days, the men were beyond desperate. They were without food and water, and their bodies were losing water fast from sweating under the hot sun. Together, they decided that unless they died beforehand, they would offer themselves as slaves to the first tribe they encountered, hoping for a reprieve in the form of sustenance. Their preeminent goal was no longer to get home or to repair the ship but just to stay alive.

Just as the men were near death, armed Arab tribesmen appeared over the horizon. When they caught sight of the dying Riley and his crew, they approached them on camelback and surrounded them with their weapons drawn.

To Riley's surprise, the subsequent acts of violence were not committed against him and his men but rather between the tribesmen, who disputed about who would get to take the American sailors captive. Fighting broke out, and several tribesmen were killed in front of the sailors, who were too weak and fatigued to do anything.

Finally, the fighting subsided as one group of the tribesmen backed off, leaving several of their comrades' bodies lying dead in the sand. The other group then captured the American sailors. In his book *Sufferings in Africa*, Riley recounted how it amazed him that the tribesmen chose to handle their disputes by killing each other rather than negotiating.

But once the conflict among them was settled, they turned their attention to the hapless and near-death Americans, who quickly found themselves torn from one another and taken away in small groups. Several of the men were beaten with clubs and chained to camels, forced to drink camel urine rather than water for sustenance.

Among the captors, a trader named Sidi Hamet and his brother claimed Riley and a few other men as prizes. Riley and his separated crew were then led away under the searing Sahara sun.

Throughout the prolonged journey, Riley grappled with the idea of committing suicide, which briefly seemed to be a tempting escape from the never-ending torment of the captors and the desert. It was only the thoughts of his wife and children back home in Connecticut that kept him alive.

Reinvigorated by his newfound determination to return home to his family, Riley decided to negotiate with his captors. He convinced Hamet to redirect his captive party toward the city of Mogador, located in present-day Essaouira in Morocco. Hamet believed Riley's story that he had a wealthy friend in the town who would pay a hefty ransom for their release.

In reality, Riley hoped they could meet more benevolent people in Mogador and perhaps even secure passage home at the city's port. Hamet warned Riley that if the reward fell short of his expectations, he would personally slit Riley's throat and keep the rest of the men captive.

The journey to Mogador was no less brutal for the men than what they had already endured. Riley and his men were repeatedly subjected to beatings during the several hundred-mile journey under the hot sun, and they were only given the bare minimum of water and food to stay alive. Their captors continued to tease them by offering them 'water,' only for it to be camel urine in reality. The harsh conditions pushed the men to the brink, resulting in staggering weight loss. Some even lost up to half their body weight.

Once they arrived in Mogador, Riley put his plan into action. He wrote a plea for salvation to his rich friend, who, again, only existed in the fabricated narrative he had given to Hamet. Addressing the letter to "The French, English, Spanish, or American Consuls," Riley implored his rich friend to purchase him and his fellow men from their enslavement and then entrusted Hamet with the letter addressed to his purported contact.

Providentially, the letter found its way into the hands of the first white man Hamet encountered: William Willshire, who was working as an assistant to the European consul. Willshire was struck by the despair and desperation conveyed in Riley's letter and made a significant and unprecedented decision: to meet Hamet's massive financial demands and secure the release of the shipwrecked captives.

Excluding two estranged crew members who would be ransomed later, the remaining captives were freed and equipped to return to the United States. Upon gaining his freedom, Riley was only barely alive. By all accounts, he was a large man who weighed more than 240 pounds at the start of the journey. By his release to Willshire, he weighed just 90 pounds.

Willshire immediately provided Riley and his men with food, water, and a place to sleep. After a few days of recovery, they embarked on a vessel to return to the United States.

Upon his return to American shores, Riley fervently dedicated himself to the cause of anti-slavery. He later chronicled what happened in his 1817 memoir *Sufferings in Africa*. The book became a bestseller with over a million copies sold. Riley's portrayal of desert wilderness survival and human bondage not only stirred the conscience of readers but also helped fuel the abolitionist cause. Among the captivated readers was a young Abraham Lincoln, who would later acknowledge *Sufferings in Africa* as one of the most influential books he ever read.

In 1822, Riley founded the Ohio town of Willshire, naming it to honor the man who saved him. Sadly, most of the men who survived the Sahara did not live long lives afterward due to the massive physical and psychological toll of their ordeal.

As for Riley, the call of the sea eventually lured him back, and he resumed working in maritime trade. Years later, he ultimately succumbed to disease on March 13, 1840, while on assignment. It was believed that his body was unable to resist the disease due to becoming severely weakened from his time as a slave in the Sahara. Most of his other crew members passed away before Riley. The last survivor was the cabin boy, the only one who defied the odds and lived to the ripe old age of 82.

———— ◆ ————

THERE IS MUCH WE can learn from the incredible ordeal of Riley and his men. Riley's narrative epitomizes the remarkable capacity of the human spirit to endure extreme conditions. Stranded in the vastness of the Sahara, Riley and his crew faced scorching daytime temperatures, freezing nights, and the physical exhaustion of traversing miles of treacherous desert terrain with little to no food and water.

Their survival hinged on their collective, unwavering resolve to press forward despite the harshness of their environment. Their survival was not due to pure luck or chance but instead to two primary factors: their determination to stay together as a team and make it out alive and Riley's negotiation skills.

Riley ensured that all decisions impacting the group were made collectively. For instance, when the men decided to venture out into the Sahara Desert to find resources when the *Commerce* could not go on any further, they decided to do it together. They stuck together the entire time, never once turning against one another. When the men were captured, Riley's negotiation skills to convince their captors to take them to Mogador was ultimately the most prominent factor in securing their release.

His negotiation and communication skills were pivotal in navigating their interactions with the Arab tribesmen and keeping them alive. When faced with the immediate threat of violence, Riley strategically engaged with the tribesmen peacefully, negotiating for his life and the safety of his crew. His ability to arrange a deal, albeit temporary, demonstrated the importance of effective communication rather than fully submitting to the will of their captors.

Riley's contemplation of committing suicide during their captivity reveals the profound mental challenges he and his crew endured. The sheer brutality of their circumstances, compounded by the constant beatings from their captors, tested their mental fortitude to its limits. Riley's ability to find a glimmer of hope amid such darkness (in his case, his desire to be reunited with his family) proves the unlimited, indomitable strength of the human mind.

The only act of 'luck' (if it could be called that) was when Riley's letter ended up in Willshire's hands. Riley, of course, did not know of any Westerners living in Mogador who could help them. The fact that the letter ended up with Willshire and that Willshire was willing and had the financial resources to secure Riley and his men's release was no doubt more than an act of luck.

It was an act of God.

From the scorching sands of the Sahara, we now journey to the icy extremes of Antarctica, where Ernest Shackleton's account of supreme endurance awaits. His expedition presents a stark contrast to Riley's desert ordeal yet echoes the same unyielding spirit of survival.

2

ENDURANCE IN ANTARCTICA

Weddell Sea off Antarctica, 1915

As we saw with Captain Riley, the Sahara Desert will test your limits like no other place on Earth, except perhaps Antarctica.

Ernest Shackleton is the most iconic figure when it comes to Antarctic exploration. He carved his legacy during the end of the Age of Exploration with a remarkable trio of expeditions to the world's formidable southernmost continent. Born in Ireland on February 15th, 1874, Shackleton embarked on a journey that would etch his name into history.

Shackleton had a lifelong fascination with the polar regions because they were two of the most unexplored places on Earth back then (and still are today). His first foray into Antarctic exploration began with his participation in the Discovery expedition, which took place from 1901 to 1904.

Subsequently, he joined the Nimrod expedition from 1907 to 1909, venturing within a mere two hundred miles from the South Pole. And although Roald Amundsen ultimately claimed the honor of reaching the pole in 1911, vast expanses of Antarctica remained uncharted.

Shackleton was undeterred by Amundsen's achievement and had a grander vision: to lead the first-ever expedition to traverse Antarctica from one side to the other. This ambitious undertaking, which came to be known as the Imperial Trans-Antarctica Expedition, was about to begin.

SURVIVING IN ANTARCTICA PRESENTS a unique set of challenges that make it one of the most inhospitable environments for humans. The continent is characterized by extreme cold, relentless winds, and vast expanses of icy terrain that never seem to end. With temperatures regularly dropping far below zero (sometimes to -40 degrees Fahrenheit), the risk of frostbite and hypothermia is an ever-present danger, day and night.

Adding to the difficulties is Antarctica's isolation. The continent is geographically remote, with vast distances separating it from other landmasses. The closest land masses are the southern tips of South America, Africa, Australia, and New Zealand, but even these are located hundreds of miles away and would take several days to reach by ship.

The lack of infrastructure and limited access means that individuals are largely on their own in emergencies, making preparedness and self-sufficiency paramount. Navigating Antarctica's harsh terrain, which includes treacherous ice sheets, hidden crevasses, and mountain ranges, requires specialized knowledge and equipment. The risk of falling into crevasses or encountering unstable ice formations underscores the perilous nature of the continent's landscape.

Antarctica has extreme wind conditions, particularly with powerful katabatic (downhill) winds exceeding 200 miles per hour. Blizzards with reduced visibility are common, making navigation difficult and increasing the risk of disorientation.

Survival in Antarctica also demands careful consideration of available resources. The lack of vegetation, arable land, and diverse wildlife means that obtaining food and sustenance is complex and resource-intensive. People attempting to survive in this barren landscape must rely on pre-stocked supplies and meticulous planning. Any survival attempt without supplies or planning is sure to result in death.

Polar wildlife, while fascinating, also poses potential dangers. Encounters with aggressive seals, territorial penguins, and large marine mammals can be hazardous at the very least. Furthermore, the continent experiences long periods of darkness during polar winters and extended daylight during summers. These extreme variations in daylight hours, coupled with the isolation and challenging conditions, can make it difficult for people to cope, sleep, and thrive in this environment.

Antarctica's hostile climate, isolation, harsh terrain, and limited resources make survival a perilous undertaking. Shackleton was acutely aware of these factors and risks when he embarked on his expeditions to the continent, but the allure of exploring the world's least-explored continent was not something he could pass by.

———————————◆———————————

ERNEST HENRY SHACKLETON WAS born on February 15, 1874 in Ireland. He was the second child in a family of ten, and his father, Henry Shackleton, engaged in farming at Kilkea.

In 1880, at six, Ernest's life took a turn when his father decided to leave farming and pursue a medical career at Trinity College Dublin. The Shackleton family, then residing in Dublin, later relocated to Sydenham in South London in 1884, where Henry practiced as a doctor for three decades.

Ernest Shackleton, having attended Dulwich College as a boy, embarked on a new journey at the age of 16 when he joined the Merchant Navy. Ten years into his maritime career, he transitioned to a different frontier by joining a British Expedition led by Captain Robert Falcon Scott, with the ambitious goal of being the first to reach the South Pole.

Shackleton's restlessness during his school years led him to pursue a career at sea. While a Royal Navy officer cadetship was an option, financial constraints and age restrictions led Shackleton to choose an apprenticeship "before the mast" aboard the square-rigged sailing ship Hoghton Tower, thanks to his father's efforts with the North Western Shipping Company.

During the next four years at sea, Shackleton honed his skills, navigating various parts of the world, building connections, and learning to engage with people from different backgrounds. In August 1894, he passed his second mate examination and assumed the role of third officer on a tramp steamer in the Welsh Shire Line.

Near the turn of the century, Shackleton achieved his first mate's ticket, and shortly thereafter, he obtained certification as a master mariner, granting him the authority to command a British ship globally.

Also around this time, Shackleton joined the Union-Castle Line, a prominent mail and passenger carrier between Britain and South Africa. Described by a shipmate as a departure from the typical young officer, Shackleton demonstrated a unique blend of sensitivity and aggression, coupled with a penchant for quoting Keats or Browning.

As the Boer War erupted in 1899 in South Africa, Shackleton moved to the troopship *Tintagel Castle*, where he crossed paths with Cedric Longstaff, the son of Llewellyn W. Longstaff, who became a key financial supporter of the upcoming British National Antarctic Expedition.

Leveraging his connection with Cedric, Shackleton secured an interview with his father, impressing him with his enthusiasm for the expedition. Longstaff recommended Shackleton to Sir Clements Markham, the expedition's overseer, resulting in Shackleton's appointment as the third officer on the expedition's ship *Discovery*, confirmed in 1901.

In June of that year, he received a commission into the Royal Navy as a sub-lieutenant in the Royal Naval Reserve. This marked the end of Shackleton's official service in the Merchant Navy, as he embarked on a new chapter in his life that would revolve around Antarctic exploration.

Shackleton engaged in the Discovery and Nimrod expeditions to Antarctica before the Imperial Trans-Antarctic Expedition, which was the expedition he would become famous for.

———— ✦ ————

THE DISCOVERY EXPEDITION FROM 1901 to 1904 marked Shackleton's first big adventure into Antarctica. Named after the *Discovery* ship, the expedition was led by Robert Falcon Scott, a recently promoted Royal Navy commander. The goal of the Discovery expedition was scientific and geographical exploration.

Despite not being a Royal Navy unit, Scott imposed the conditions of the Naval Discipline Act on the crew, officers, and scientific staff, aligning the ship and expedition with Royal Navy standards.

Shackleton, though inclined towards a more informal leadership style based on his background and instincts, accepted this approach. His designated responsibilities included overseeing sea-water analysis, serving as the ward-room caterer, managing the holds, stores, and provisions, and organizing entertainment for the crew.

Discovery embarked on its Antarctic journey from London's East India Docks on July 31, 1901. After stops in South Africa and New Zealand, it reached the Antarctic coast on January 9, 1902. Shackleton engaged in various activities throughout the Antarctic winter of 1902, and he was regarded as the most popular officer among the crew due to his sociability and charisma.

Scott selected Shackleton to join him and Edward Wilson on the southern journey, aiming to achieve the highest latitude towards the South Pole. Although not a direct attempt on the Pole, reaching a high latitude held significance. The expedition set out on November 2, 1902.

Their southern journey faced challenges, including the poor performance of the dogs that carried their supplies, leading to the rapid sickness and eventual death of some of the dogs. The men encountered snow blindness, frostbite, and scurvy during the march, with all three suffering from these conditions. Shackleton, in particular, experienced a physical breakdown on the return journey and could not contribute his share of the work.

By the time they reached the ship on February 3, 1903, Shackleton was severely weakened. Diary entries from other men on the expedition noted Shackleton's worsening health, marked by shortness of breath, constant coughing, and undisclosed symptoms. A medical examination yielded inconclusive results, prompting Scott to send Shackleton home on the relief ship *Morning*.

After receiving the necessary rest, medical care, and recovery, three years later, on August 7, 1907, Shackleton led the Nimrod ship from England and commenced the British Antarctic Expedition, less formally known as the Nimrod Expedition.

The Nimrod expedition reached New Zealand at the end of November and, after final preparations, set sail from Lyttelton Harbour on January 1, 1908, en route to the Antarctic. Shackleton's initial plan involved utilizing the old Discovery base in McMurdo Sound to launch attempts on the South Pole and South Magnetic Pole.

However, before Shackleton departed England, Scott had pressured him out of establishing himself in the McMurdo area, which Scott considered his exclusive field of work. Reluctantly, Shackleton agreed to seek winter quarters at the Barrier Inlet, briefly visited in 1902 on Discovery, or King Edward VII Land.

To conserve coal, a steamer ship towed the *Nimrod* 1,650 miles to the Antarctic ice, with Shackleton successfully securing cost-sharing from the New Zealand government and the Union Steamship Company. Adhering to his commitment to Scott, the ship headed for the eastern sector of the Great Ice Barrier, arriving there in late January 1908. They made a significant discovery—the Barrier Inlet had expanded to create a large bay teeming with hundreds of whales. In response, they named it the "Bay of Whales."

The Nimrod expedition faced challenging ice conditions, rendering the establishment of a safe base at the Barrier Inlet unfeasible. Despite an extended search for anchorage at King Edward VII Land, no suitable location was found. Shackleton, compelled by practical considerations such as ice pressure, coal shortage, and the absence of a known alternative base nearby, had to break his commitment to Scott.

The *Nimrod* then set sail for McMurdo Sound, reaching it on January 29, but was halted by ice 16 miles north of Discovery's old base at Hut Point. After weather-related delays, a base was established at Cape Royds, approximately 24 miles north of Hut Point. Despite challenging conditions, Shackleton's ability to connect with his crew fostered a positive and focused atmosphere.

In October, Shackleton and three companions—Frank Wild, Eric Marshall, and Jameson Adams—embarked on the "Great Southern Journey." They reached an area that was 112 miles from the Pole. During this journey, they discovered the Beardmore Glacier, named after Shackleton's patron, and became the first individuals to observe and traverse the South Polar Plateau.

The return to McMurdo Sound became a race against starvation, and the party endured half-rations for a significant duration. At one critical point, Shackleton sacrificed his daily biscuit for the ailing Frank Wild, leaving a lasting impact on the entire party. They returned to Hut Point just in time to catch the ship and leave.

The Discovery and Nimrod expeditions both provided Shackleton with the vital experience he would need to lead his expedition into the Antarctic region years later.

Upon his return home, he received significant public honors. King Edward VII received him in July of 1909, and Shackleton was elevated to a Commander of the Royal Victorian Order. In November, he was knighted, becoming Sir Ernest Shackleton.

Shackleton immersed himself in a demanding schedule of public appearances, lectures, and social engagements. Eager to capitalize on his newfound celebrity, he ventured into the business world with ambitious plans, but he was unsuccessful.

He also could not resist the temptation of returning to Antarctica. He began to plan a new expedition, one that he would lead himself.

In December 1913, Shackleton unveiled the details of his ambitious new expedition, appropriately named the "Imperial Trans-Antarctic Expedition."

———— ✦ ————

THE MEN WHO EMBARKED on the Imperial Trans-Antarctic Expedition expected to cross Antarctica from one end to the other. In reality, they would never set foot on the continent itself and would instead become locked into the most significant battle for survival of their lives.

Planning for the journey began in 1909 once Shackleton returned from the Nimrod expedition. He planned to set sail on the *Endurance,* a Norwegian-built three-mast schooner that was the most durable wooden ship then, and travel from the southern tip of South America to Antarctica before crossing the southern continent and ending up in Australia or New Zealand.

Endurance, originally named *Polaris,* was built for tourist cruises in the Arctic. Shackleton purchased the ship after securing funds for the exploration, gave it a new name, and repurposed it for exploration.

By the time the expedition launched, however, World War I had broken out in Europe. Faced with this, Shackleton offered *Endurance* to the British Navy to aid in the war effort against Germany, but the government allowed him to proceed with the expedition anyway. The government believed that a successful crossing of Antarctica would help boost British morale for the war.

In total, there were twenty-eight men aboard the *Endurance* when they departed.

Unfortunately, it turned out to be an unusually icy year in Antarctica. In a twist of fate, Shackleton was forced to bring *Endurance* to a pause at South Georgia, an island that Captain James Cook had discovered in the 1700s. During this hiatus, the crew forged bonds with Norwegian whalers who lived on the island and who no doubt recognized *Endurance* as a Norwegian vessel.

As the icy grip loosened, Shackleton and his crew set sail anew, reinforced with additional coal reserves that would prove crucial for piercing the formidable pack ice in the Weddell Sea. A laborious six-week odyssey followed, during which the crew chartered a course through over a thousand miles of pack ice.

The crew, fueled by determination, triumphantly neared their destination, closing in to within a mere hundred miles of reaching the continent. But this jubilation was short-lived as disaster unfurled. The pack ice had grown thicker and created an insurmountable barricade around the *Endurance*.

On January 18, 1915, the ice closed in from all sides, ensnaring the *Endurance* and rendering it motionless. Shackleton and his crew were now trapped.

———◆———

BY THIS POINT, THE goal was not to cross Antarctica but to stay alive.

Despite Shackleton's profound disappointment in the unfolding events, his crew held him in high esteem. It was their belief in Shackleton's abilities to lead them out that kept them together and prevented them from turning against one another.

Shackleton knew that he needed to maintain their respect and, more crucially, safeguard their lives by projecting confidence and decisiveness in his actions.

As the ice followed a southwest drift, the *Endurance* moved along with it. The crew toiled day after day to free the ship, but whenever cracks in the hull appeared, they were compelled to withdraw from their efforts as the ice continued its relentless journey.

By February, reality had fully set in. Sub-zero temperatures had imprisoned the ship, condemning the men to endure frigid winter months. Any hope that they could free the *Endurance* was now vanquished.

With the onset of winter, the region was plunged into long nights. To pass the time, the men engaged in activities like football and hockey on the ice. Their only hope was to wait for spring or summer when the air would warm, and hopefully, enough ice would melt to free the ship.

Months passed, and it was not until July that the sun and daylight returned. However, relentless blizzards forced the men into shelters to battle the biting cold. Shackleton realized that the *Endurance* would soon succumb to the crushing force of the encroaching ice and break apart.

Running low on provisions, the crew turned to hunting seals and penguins for sustenance, having drifted almost twelve hundred miles from their original position. They were now located approximately 350 miles from Paulet Island, the closest place with essential resources.

Sure enough, by October of 1915, the ice's relentless pressure began to crush the *Endurance*. The stern post twisted, creating a breach in the ship's hull. The crew swiftly climbed aboard, engaging water pumps in a desperate bid to force out the invading water.

Acknowledging the vessel's inevitable fate, Shackleton ordered the evacuation of all provisions, supplies, and lifeboats from the doomed ship and the establishment of a makeshift camp on the ice, which would become known as "Ocean Camp."

In November, the *Endurance* finally succumbed to the ice's overwhelming forces and sank beneath the frigid waters. Fortunately, a significant portion of supplies and equipment was salvaged before the vessel's demise, thanks to Shackleton's instructions to strip the ship of anything useful.

Isolated from communication with the outside world and facing diminishing resources, the stranded men faced yet another physical test. Spring would soon hit, causing the ice to break apart gradually. While this would be a cause for celebration if the *Endurance* were still afloat, it now meant constant vigilance as the ground beneath their feet became increasingly precarious.

Shackleton deemed it time to abandon the camp and search for dry land, ideally near Paulet Island. The men were equipped with three lifeboats rescued from the Endurance: the James Caird, the Dudley Docker, and the Stancomb Wills. Each lifeboat was about twenty feet long.

Navigating the treacherous terrain, the men alternated between hauling the boats over ice and through open water when the ice became too thin. Despite their intensive efforts, the drifting sea ice limited their progress to a mere thirty miles from their initial location.

Months later, the men finally reached Elephant Island, the first dry land they had seen since South Georgia. This reignited a spark of hope in each of them. They established a camp that they named Point Wild and found refuge by using their lifeboats as shelter.

In a seemingly hopeless situation with no ships in sight and no means of communication, Shackleton announced to the men that rescue was impossible.

Faced with no alternative, he dared to dispatch a lifeboat with a small crew to the nearest populated area, the whaling station at South Georgia, where they had spent time with the Norwegian whalers. The island, however, was over eight hundred miles away, with lots of ice and 50-foot waves serving as obstacles.

With no modern navigational aids, they relied on the sun to guide their way. Leaving Frank Wild in command on Elephant Island, Shackleton informed the men that if no rescue came from him by spring, they should aim for Deception Island, which whalers frequented.

Setting forth in the *James Caird* on April 24, 1916, Shackleton and five crew members valiantly faced the harsh elements in their pursuit of salvation. Despite the small size of the vessel and the relentless sea, they managed to cover an impressive 70 miles per day. The constant seawater spray forced them to move forward with soaking-wet clothing, blankets, and sleeping bags.

The accumulation of thick ice on the boat added to their problems, which forced the men to employ makeshift tools to chip it away. Beyond the physical toll, the weight of the ice posed a danger to the vessel.

After a week of freezing seawater and frostbite, a breakthrough emerged. The sun broke through the clouds, providing rare warmth to Shackleton and his men. They calculated they were over halfway to South Georgia as the ice began to recede. As the air grew warmer, the sight of seabirds signaled they were getting closer to dry land. Two weeks after departing Elephant Island, the crew finally laid eyes on the recognizable island of South Georgia.

———— ♦ ————

SHACKLETON'S ORDEAL WAS STILL far from over. Navigating through reefs, battling high winds, and maneuvering through shallow rocks along the coast proved an arduous challenge for him and the *James Caird* crew. After multiple attempts and more than a day of effort, they safely guided their small boat into a cove.

After setting foot on land, they had the daunting task of traversing over 20 miles of glaciers, rocky terrain, and treacherous mountains to reach the nearest known whaling station.

After days of hiking, including rappelling down rocky terrains, the exhausted crew finally spotted a whaling boat entering a bay. They descended the side of a waterfall, becoming even more drenched to the skin. When they reached the bottom, they walked into the Stromness whaling station.

Shackleton and the other five men shocked the whalers with their matted hair, tattered clothes, and unkempt appearances, but they wasted no time coordinating with them to rescue the remaining 22 men on Elephant Island. They initially set off in the British whaling ship *Southern Sky* and made it back to the Falkland Islands off the coast of Argentina.

Their initial attempt to rescue the men with the Uruguayan government's ship *Instituto de Pesca* failed. They then turned to a chartered ship, the Emma, but the second rescue attempt failed when the engine broke down. Forced to try a third vessel, Shackleton and his men borrowed the steam tug *Yelcho* from the Chilean government.

Finally, on August 30, 1916, the *Yelcho* successfully pushed through the ice, reaching Elephant Island and rescuing the stranded men. Incredibly, each of them was still alive.

———————◆———————

NOT ONE MAN OF Shackleton's crew was lost during their incredible ordeal. The men had braved the loss of their ship, non-stop freezing temperatures, the cold spray of water, and brutal snowstorms for over two years.

In hindsight, it's easy to see precisely why they survived: they stuck together. The men were united by a shared belief in Shackleton's decision-making abilities. They never once turned against him or each other, and they worked as a team to build shelter, hunt for food, and keep warm.

Their survival underscores the triumph of human spirit, leadership, and working as a team in any survival situation. If you ever find yourself in a survival situation with other people, work together, share resources, and stay together.

Shackleton and the five other men only physically separated themselves from the rest of the crew once it became apparent that rescue would not be arriving, and even then, Shackleton gave the rest of the men a backup plan to make for Deception Island in the event he wasn't able to rescue them.

While Shackleton may not have achieved his initial goal of crossing the Antarctic, his exceptional leadership skills played a massive role in keeping his men united and ensuring that no lives were lost during their tumultuous journey. The survival saga of Shackleton and his crew over two years in the unforgiving Antarctic landscape stands today as one of the most awe-inspiring tales of real-life endurance.

The experience did not discourage Shackleton from living a life of on-going adventure. Aiming to return to Antarctica in 1921, during his fourth expedition to the continent, his journey was cut short at 47 by a heart attack while his ship was anchored at South Georgia Island. With Shackleton's passing, the age of Antarctic Exploration grew to a close, but the incredible story of how he led his crew to survival still lives on.

Now, having braved the Antarctic's formidable challenges with Shackleton and his crew, we'll shift our focus to the Pacific and Japan, where Louis Zamperini's gripping account of survival is about to unfold.

3

RESILIENCE IN JAPANESE JUNGLES

South Pacific Ocean, 1943

Louis Zamperini's tale of survival is nothing short of extraordinary. It's one of the most remarkable survival stories not only of the Second World War but of all time. While serving as a bombardier in the U.S. Army Air Forces (as it was named then), Zamperini's plane crashed into the Pacific Ocean during a rescue mission in 1943. What followed was a 47-day ordeal adrift at sea with only two other survivors battling starvation, dehydration, and the constant threat of sharks.

The sheer tenacity and will to live that Zamperini and his fellow survivors displayed in the vast expanse of the Pacific Ocean are awe-inspiring in and of themselves. But his story would take an even more harrowing turn when he and his comrades, already near death from being adrift at sea for so long, were captured by the Japanese Navy. As a prisoner of war, Zamperini faced brutal treatment, torture, and deprivation for over two years until the war's end.

Yet, even in the face of relentless adversity, his resilience shone through. His ability to endure years of mistreatment, maintain his spirit, and ultimately survive until his liberation by American forces with a profound sense of forgiveness and redemption is incredible. Zamperini transcended the physical aspect of survival and vividly demonstrated how mental strength, fortitude, resilience, and the power of forgiveness can help one survive.

———— ◆ ————

ZAMPERINI WAS BORN ON January 26, 1917, in Olean, New York, before relocating to California during his childhood. It was in Torrance High School that he discovered his innate talent for running, which helped him persevere since he was often bullied for his Italian heritage. He emerged as a remarkable athlete, showcasing his prowess on the track by setting a national high school mile record at 4:21.2, which stood unbroken for 19 years. This early success paved the way for his athletic pursuits at the University of Southern California (USC).

At USC, Zamperini's running skills continued to shine. His achievements in track and field earned him a spot on the U.S. track and field team for the 1936 Summer Olympics held in Berlin, Germany. In this international arena, Zamperini competed in the 5,000-meter race, representing our nation on the global stage. Though he didn't secure a medal, his performance garnered attention, even leading to a personal meeting request from Adolf Hitler.

Zamperini's early life, marked by a journey from Olean to California and his exceptional athletic achievements in high school and college, set the stage for the subsequent chapters of his extraordinary life. These formative years, characterized by his physical and mental resilience, laid the foundation for the challenges awaiting him once America entered World War II.

◆

AFTER ENLISTING IN THE United States Army Air Force in September 1941, Louis Zamperini earned a commission as a second lieutenant and was stationed on the Pacific island of Funafuti. He then became a bombardier on the B-24 Liberator bomber "Super Man."

During a bombing mission against the Japanese-held island of Nauru in April 1943, Super Man faced a fierce attack from three Japanese Zero fighter planes. The bomber sustained severe damage, leaving five crew members wounded and one dead. Despite the perilous situation, Zamperini's actions, which included administering first aid to the injured crew members, ultimately saved the lives of two of them during the return flight.

With Super Man deemed unfit for flight, Zamperini and the remaining healthy crew members were reassigned to search for a lost aircraft and crew. Assigned to another B-24, known among pilots as the problematic "Green Hornet," Zamperini and his crewmates faced even more challenging conditions. Mechanical difficulties led the Green Hornet to crash into the ocean 850 miles south of Oahu in May 1943.

Eight of the 11 men on board lost their lives, but Zamperini, along with pilots Russell Allen Phillips and Francis McNamara, miraculously survived the crash and found themselves adrift at sea. Facing starvation and shark attacks, the survivors subsisted on rainwater, raw fish, and birds.

After 33 days at sea, tragedy struck when McNamara succumbed to the harsh conditions. Zamperini and Phillips, left with no choice, respectfully wrapped McNamara's body and released it into the ocean. Their chances of survival appeared quite remote.

———— ◆ ————

NAVIGATING TREACHEROUS WATERS, ZAMPERINI and Phillips were confronted by typhoon-sized waves, relentless heat from the sun, and strafing gunfire from Japanese fighter planes overhead, though each bullet miraculously missed them. On July 15, their emaciated bodies were rescued - but not by Americans. Instead, it was Japanese soldiers who took them aboard a ship.

Bound at the hands and tethered to the mast, Zamperini and Phillips faced taunts and beatings from their captors. Thankfully, a compassionate turn occurred when the ship's captain intervened, ordering the men to be untied and provided with water and a biscuit – their first sustenance in over a week. It was perhaps the generosity of this Japanese captain that kept Zamperini and Phillips alive since both were near death at this point.

The survivors were transported to an island and underwent a thorough examination and treatment for their wounds. The startling revelation came when their pre-flight weights of 150 to 160 pounds were contrasted with their current states, having lost half their weight during the harrowing ordeal. Zamperini recalled that upon confirming their drastic weight loss, he realized how narrowly he had escaped death.

In addition to the medical care they received, Zamperini and Phillips were offered plentiful food, alcohol, and cigarettes. Relocated to a room, they recounted their survival story to Japanese officials who interrogated them, discovering they had drifted an astonishing two thousand miles to the Marshall Islands. Their battered raft bore no less than 48 bullet holes.

For a bit, the two men thought they would be treated well. They had warm beds to sleep in, and food and water were provided to them daily. But their relief quickly turned to apprehension when they learned they were being transferred to another atoll on Kwajalein. This island was notorious among American ranks as "Execution Island," and Zamperini knew full well what lay ahead.

———— ◆ ————

DURING THEIR JOURNEY TO Kwajalein, Japanese soldiers displayed a friendly demeanor toward the Americans, ensuring their well-being by providing hearty meals and separate sleeping quarters. Zamperini was surprised by this seeming hospitality since he was fully aware of the reputation the Japanese on Kwajalein had for treating American prisoners. However, as the freighter approached the island, the atmosphere dramatically shifted.

On July 16, a pivotal day in their captivity, the dynamics drastically changed almost overnight. Blindfolded and carried off the freighter in a fireman's carry, Zamperini and Phillips found themselves unceremoniously thrown into cells with minimal space for a single occupant. Their cells were tainted by bug infestations and offered only a small square window in the door for ventilation. The air inside was stifling, sweltering, and tainted by the pungency emanating from the floor latrine.

Within the confines of his cell, Zamperini discovered a chilling engraving on one of the walls. It recounted the fate of "Nine marines marooned on Makin Island, August 18, 1942," with the names of the men etched beneath it. Zamperini, familiar with their story like most American soldiers, knew these marines had been inadvertently left behind after an attack and had seemingly vanished. Recognizing their names was ominous.

As Zamperini absorbed the stark reality of his surroundings, his emaciated form, and the dire circumstances, an overwhelming wave of emotion overcame him. Muffling his sobs with his hands each day, he grappled with the harshness of his new reality. The transition from the initial amicable treatment by the Japanese on the journey to the sudden oppressive conditions of their cells marked a poignant turning point in his harrowing experience, and it would only get worse for the duration of the war.

For a grueling 42 days, Zamperini and Phillips endured an agonizing ordeal on Kwajalein, surpassing the hardships they faced on the raft. At times, Zamperini found himself yearning for death as the relentless torment at the hands of his Japanese captors unfolded. He realized he was perhaps better off adrift in the ocean than to have been 'rescued' by the Japanese.

Each day, the two men were provided a meager ration of sustenance – a golf ball-sized dry biscuit and a swallow of scalding brown water. The biscuit, callously thrown through the window, shattered on the ground, forcing Louie to scramble for the scattered crumbs like a desperate rodent. The revelation of the Marines' execution heightened the dread, as Zamperini lived with the constant anticipation of being pulled from his cell and killed either by rifle or katana.

The guards on Kwajalein reveled in surpassing each other with acts of cruelty. Zamperini's pleas for water were met with scalding hot liquid thrown in his face. Long sticks poked and prodded him through the window, and he was compelled to dance while enduring a barrage of stones. The guards often added a macabre touch by slicing their hands across their throats, accompanied by laughter, taunting Zamperini with execution. Zamperini suffered nightmares each night and woke up each morning believing that it would be his last.

Twice, a submarine docked near the island, unleashing more than 80 Japanese soldiers who took turns subjecting Zamperini and Phillips to further abuse. They hurled stones and sharp sticks at them, along with spitting on them and kicking their bodies on the floor. Unable to communicate, Zamperini and Phillips resorted to scuffing sounds on the floor, signaling their survival to one another.

Both Zamperini and Phillips found themselves removed from their cells multiple times, with each instance heightening the fear of impending execution. To their surprise, one time, they were instead led to an interrogation room. There, they faced questions about the logistics of American bombers and base sites in Hawaii. Zamperini, revealing as much truth as he dared, discreetly pointed out the decoy base sites in Hawaii that the U.S. forces had created to mislead Japanese bombers.

On four separate occasions, the two were escorted to the infirmary and subjected to harrowing medical experiments. Injected with solutions that induced dizziness and agonizing pain and covered them in rashes, their survival was nothing short of miraculous. Zamperini noticed that many other POWs who underwent similar experiments did not survive the ordeal, and he wondered for the rest of his life afterward how he was able to survive when the others had not.

Eventually, the duo received news of their transfer to an official POW camp in Japan. Zamperini clung to a newfound hope, anticipating access to Red Cross supplies and the possibility of reconnecting with their families. The transfer also hopefully meant a reprieve from the looming threat of execution.

Zamperini did not imagine that things could get worse. He was wrong.

———— ♦ ————

FOLLOWING A THREE-WEEK JOURNEY by sea, Louie and Phil found themselves at Ofuna, a secret POW camp in Japan that the Americans were not aware of. Upon arrival, Zamperini was granted his first bath since leaving Hawaii. He was led to a room where he was shocked to be reunited with his old friend Jimmie Sasaki, whom he had befriended at the University of Southern California.

Unaware of the suspicions and investigations surrounding Jimmie back home, Louie was bewildered to encounter him in a prison camp. Their conversation, which spanned USC memories and Jimmie's boasts about his high-ranking position in the Japanese military, lasted for an extended period.

After talking with Jimmie, Zamperini was taken to the yard, where he joined 200 fellow prisoners.

His time at Ofuna proved to be a nightmarish chapter in his POW experience. Unregistered as an official POW camp, Ofuna operated outside the purview of the Red Cross, evading the regulations of the Geneva Convention meant to safeguard prisoners of war. Instead, the camp adhered to a set of rules designed to break and humiliate their captives.

The strict guidelines set by the camp commandants governed every aspect of camp life. Prisoners were prohibited from speaking or making eye contact with each other, and their eyes were to remain cast down at all times. Learning the Japanese language became imperative for understanding instructions. Each day commenced with *tenko*, or roll call, and any deviation from these regulations resulted in severe beatings in front of the other prisoners.

The guards were also allowed to unleash vicious beatings at their discretion. Employing clubs as their weapons of choice, the guards escalated their brutality for any attempt prisoners made to defend themselves or assist others.

Over the months, the emaciated prisoners faced starvation, exacerbated by guards pillaging their food shipments meant for sustenance. Rations amounted to putrid broth and contaminated rice, devoid of any nutritional value. The prevalence of dysentery added to their misery, and Zamperini became reduced to a skeletal figure even worse than when he was adrift at sea. Despite Jimmie's frequent visits, Zamperini found no solace, and he noted how Jimmie continued to focus on reminiscing about USC. Zamperini realized Jimmie was friendly with him only so that Zamperini could reveal information about the American positions.

Looking back on the ordeal, Zamperini claimed that he had only survived Ofuna because of the secret assistance of two kitchen aides who discreetly provided him with extra rice balls.

But now, the worst part of his imprisonment was about to begin.

Zamperini was transported to yet another POW camp, this time to one called Omori, which was situated on an artificial island in Tokyo Bay and connected to the main city by a bamboo-slat bridge. The disciplinary measures at Omori were ruthlessly enforced by Japanese corporal Mutsuhiro Watanabe, a figure whose wrath spared no one and was known as "The Bird."

Arriving in the winter of 1943, Watanabe swiftly gained notoriety as one of the most feared guards in the Japanese military. His relentless tactics earned Omori the grim nickname of "punishment camp."

Hailing from an affluent and privileged family, Watanabe was sophisticated despite his brutality. He pursued a degree in French literature at university, and after graduating in 1942, he relocated to Tokyo to work in a newsroom. With the outbreak of war with the United States, Watanabe abandoned his job and enlisted in the military, harboring ambitions of becoming an officer like his brother.

Despite his privileged background and education, Watanabe faced disappointment when he was repeatedly passed over for promotions, being informed that he would never ascend beyond the rank of corporal. He transferred the pure rage and anger from this news to the cruel way he treated his prisoners, which included reportedly ordering a prisoner to endure nightly face punches for three weeks, subjecting an appendectomy patient to judo practice, and forcing another prisoner to endure four days in a shack wearing only underwear during winter.

But his most prized captive by far was Zamperini, who he beat and tormented more than any other prisoner. Watanabe would sadistically have the guards beat Zamperini repeatedly in front of the other prisoners and then make the other prisoners beat Zamperini in turn. These beatings came when Zamperini's work performance in the camp did not meet the strict standards Watanabe set, or sometimes even for no reason.

Zamperini suffered from vomiting and an alarming physical symptom, as his fingers left indentations when pressed against his legs. Zamperini recognized this as the onset of beriberi, a life-threatening vitamin B deficiency.

Everything changed for the better in August of 1945. Watanabe began making trips away from the camp, and the non-stop violence and beatings abruptly ceased when the Japanese guards vanished, leaving the POWs in uncertainty about what was happening.

On the morning of August 20th, the camp commander gathered the seven hundred POWs in the yard, announcing the cessation of hostilities between Allied and Japanese forces. For the first time, the prisoners were permitted to bathe in the nearby river. Zamperini, alongside the others, stumbled into the water and collapsed. A sudden rumble in the sky signaled the approach of a bomber, and the men were elated to see American symbols on its side. The plane dropped supplies, including food, water, bars of chocolate, cartons of cigarettes, and a note promising further deliveries to the jubilant cheers of the men below.

Zamperini's harrowing experiences as a POW were now over.

ZAMPERINI'S STORY AFTER WORLD War II is no less remarkable than when he was stranded at sea and at the mercy of the Japanese.

He was initially declared missing in action and later presumed killed in action by the United States military, and his return home was met with a hero's welcome. His immediate post-war struggles led him to a dark period of heavy drinking in an attempt to erase the haunting memories.

A turning point in Zamperini's life came through the influence of his wife, Cynthia Applewhite, who embraced Christianity after attending one of Billy Graham's evangelistic events. Reluctantly attending a similar gathering in 1949, Zamperini found that Graham's preaching resonated deeply with him.

After acknowledging Jesus Christ as his savior and Lord, Louis Zamperini embarked on a new calling as a Christian evangelist. Forgiveness was a recurring theme in his message, and his later years were marked by acts of forgiveness and reconciliation. He found and visited former guards from his POW days, expressing forgiveness and even witnessing some of their lives transformed by Christ.

Throughout his senior years, Zamperini continued to engage his life with vigor. He proved he still had the spirit and the physicality of an athlete in him when he ran a leg in the 1998 Olympic Torch Relay in Nagano, Japan, just days before his 81st birthday. He passed away in 2014 at the age of 97.

What makes Zamperini's tale incredibly inspiring is his ability to find hope and forgiveness, even in the darkest corners of human experience. Despite enduring two years of physical and psychological torture as a prisoner of war, Zamperini showed what compassion and reconciliation are all about when he extended forgiveness to his captors and continued to preach the Gospel for the rest of his life. Watanabe, however, refused to meet him and died in 2003. Before Watanabe passed away, Zamperini sent a letter to him, forgiving him for his mistreatment during the war. It is unknown if Watanabe ever received or read the letter.

Zamperini's story exceeds one of mere physical survival. His experiences and subsequent actions beautifully demonstrated that even after suffering unimaginable abuse, when one truly grasps the forgiveness that's been extended to them, they can, in turn, forgive others of their wrongdoings.

And perhaps such a transformation of the human heart requires the most remarkable courage.

Zamperini is not the only person who survived an extended time in a jungle. We now turn to the remarkable survival story of a young woman who endured a harrowing ordeal in the Amazon rainforest, further exploring themes of resilience and the will to survive in extreme conditions.

4

TWO-MILE FALL FROM THE PERUVIAN SKY

Amazon Jungle in Central Peru, 1971

Juliane Koepcke embarked on LANSA Flight 508 on December 24, 1971, without any idea of the ordeal that awaited her. Amid the chaos of the plane wreckage hurtling towards the Earth, the 17-year-old found herself strapped to a row of seats, plummeting uncontrollably. As the ground approached at a rate of almost 150 feet per second, she managed a fleeting thought – the dense Peruvian rainforest resembled heads of broccoli.

A fierce thunderstorm had ravaged the plane, and Juliane, still attached to her seat, tumbled through the air. Before losing consciousness, she believed her glimpse of the Amazon trees would mark the end. To her astonishment, Juliane awoke to find the jungle canopy above her. It was now Christmas Day. Clad in a torn, sleeveless mini-dress with one sandal, she miraculously survived a 1.9-mile fall from the sky with relatively minor injuries.

However, her battle for survival had only just begun. Stranded in the perilous Peruvian jungle, inhabited by venomous snakes, mosquitoes, and spiders, Juliane faced the daunting puzzle of navigating back to civilization. This resilient young woman, the daughter of renowned zoologists who had taught her survival skills, had to rely on those lessons and her resourcefulness to endure and emerge from the absolutely harrowing experience.

———◆———

THE AMAZON RAINFOREST IS one of the toughest regions in the entire world to survive in. It may not be as cold as Antarctica or as arid as the Sahara, but it's just as vast and comes with its unique survival challenges. Dense vegetation makes navigation difficult; the extreme biodiversity of venomous or otherwise dangerous creatures poses real threats; and the non-stop rain (during the wet season) coupled with the heat brings stifling humidity.

The unforgiving terrain consists of towering trees and thick undergrowth. Knowing where to go without proper tools is an arduous task, and effectively traversing this dense landscape requires expertise in identifying pathways and avoiding potential hazards.

The Amazon's diverse wildlife adds another layer of difficulty to survival. With numerous venomous snakes, large predators like jaguars, and swarms of insects and mosquitoes, individuals must be constantly vigilant to minimize potentially dangerous encounters.

The rainforest's hot and humid climate, along with persistent rainfall, creates an environment conducive to the proliferation of diseases. Malaria, dengue fever, and other tropical illnesses pose a constant health risk. Maggots can also become a severe problem if you sustain any open wounds on your body that could then become infected.

What makes surviving in the Amazon Rainforest more frustrating is that resources are abundant, yet obtaining them without proper expertise is challenging. Finding clean water, identifying suitable food sources, and constructing adequate shelter requires a deep understanding of the ecosystem. For example, water is everywhere in the rainforest, in streams, rivers, groundwater, and rainwater.

Boiling water to purify it of harmful bacteria can be very difficult if you do not have any fire-starting devices with you. Disorientation, combined with a lack of water and the overbearing hot and humid environment, would also be a constant concern in the Amazon.

The Amazon's isolation and vastness contribute further to its difficulty. Due to navigational problems, it's easy to walk around in circles, and even if you do manage to walk in a fairly straight line, it could take weeks, if not months, before you walk out because of how expansive the rainforest is. The lack of critical infrastructure throughout the rainforest, such as roads or communication networks, exacerbates the challenge of seeking emergency assistance.

Cultural preferences and practices also add a layer of complexity to survival in the Amazon. The rainforest is home to various indigenous communities, each with unique customs and social structures—some of whom have had limited contact with elements of the Western world. If you stumble upon a remote tribal village or a hunting party, it would be a coin flip whether the tribal members try to help you out of curiosity or to dispense with you outright.

Even people with extensive survival skills and experiences find the challenges of the Amazon Rainforest incredibly complex and daunting. But Juliane Koepcke managed to survive here for nearly two weeks with little more than the clothes on her back — *after* having sustained injuries from her fall. Let's find out how she did it.

———— ◆ ————

JULIANE KOEPCK WAS BORN in Lima, Peru on October 10, 1954. She was an only child, and her parents engaged in work at Lima's Museum of Natural History during her childhood.

Her father, Hans-Wilhelm Koepcke, achieved renown as a zoologist, while her mother, Maria Koepcke, focused on tropical bird research. Together, they established the Panguana biological research station, an endeavor that allowed them to dive into researching the intricacies of the lush rainforest ecosystem.

At age 14, Juliane accompanied her parents as they left Lima to establish Panguana in the Amazon rainforest. Growing up on the station, Juliane described herself as a "jungle child," gaining profound insights into rainforest life and debunking the perception of it as a perilous environment.

Contrary to the belief that the rainforest is a "green hell," Juliane found it not too dangerous. It was in the jungle that she acquired the crucial survival skills that would keep her alive during her upcoming survival ordeal. Her education was unconventional, initially being homeschooled at Panguana. However, she eventually returned to Lima, the Peruvian capital, to complete her formal education.

Juliane embarked on that fateful flight with her mother from Lima, Peru, to the city of Pucallpa in the Amazonian rainforest. Their purpose was to visit her father, who worked in the rainforest. Juliane likewise aspired to study zoology, following in her parents' footsteps.

In her recollection of the ill-fated flight years later, Juliane detailed the initially uneventful 30 minutes of the journey, with passengers being served snacks. The atmosphere changed dramatically when the aircraft entered a thunderstorm, and lightning illuminated the turbulent surroundings. Chaos ensued in the cabin, with people screaming and crying as the plane was tossed about.

Despite the unsettling conditions, Juliane's mother, a nervous flier, tried to offer reassurance, expressing hope that everything would be alright. The situation took a dire turn when the plane entered a nosedive, accompanied by the ominous words from her mother, "Now it's all over."

As the plane disintegrated mid-air, Juliane, still strapped to her seat, became detached from the wreckage. The next moment, she found herself violently hurtling 10,000 feet toward the jungle canopy below.

While still in the air, she lost consciousness and regained it seconds later, now upside-down. Upon impact, she lost consciousness again, only regaining awareness the following day around 9 A.M. She had many visible injuries, including deep cuts, a broken collarbone, an eye injury, and a concussion. Her watch, remarkably still working, indicated the time.

Despite the pain and disorientation, she lay there in a vulnerable position throughout the remainder of the day and the subsequent night until the next morning.

Deprived of her glasses, Juliane struggled with orientation. Her immediate concern was to locate her mother, Maria. The strong bond and shared passion for the natural world that Maria had instilled in her daughter would become a guiding force in Juliane's fight for survival. Despite her weakened state, Juliane desperately searched for her mother's whereabouts, but to no avail.

Despite the concussion-induced fog in her head, Juliane could distinguish the croaks of frogs and the calls of birds around her. The familiarity of these sounds reassured her that she was in a jungle she recognized — from the Panguana region.

Realizing she was not far from home, Juliane knew the importance of navigating the dense rainforest correctly so she wouldn't walk around in circles. Drawing upon the extensive knowledge her parents had imparted to her about the jungle, she mentally retraced this information, determined to find the right path despite the challenges of her concussion. With great effort, she freed herself from the remnants of the plane seat.

In the following 11 days, Juliane summoned her survival instincts. Familiar with her surroundings' dangers, she navigated the rugged terrain, hoping for rescue.

Her recollecting her father's guidance to search for water and follow its course to a human settlement would prove pivotal. She discovered a small spring, providing her with a crucial source of drinking water. Beyond hydration, the spring also served as a navigational aid, offering her a path to follow. Juliane decided to follow the stream through the jungle. Eventually, the stream fed into a larger river. Believing the river could lead her to safety, she continued her journey through the dense Amazon Rainforest.

———————— ◆ ————————

JULIANE INITIATED HER GRUELING journey downstream. She was so accustomed to the jungle that the Amazon felt like home. As she navigated through the dense terrain, she alternated between walking and swimming to cover the distance.

She also noticed rescue planes and helicopters flying overhead. Despite her attempts to attract their attention, she remained unnoticed, and she felt as if she would never be found.

Juliane took calculated measures to navigate the challenging environment. Her father's warning about the dangers of sharp-toothed piranhas in shallow waters led her to stay in the deeper parts of the stream where the risk was lower.

However, the relentless rain during the jungle's wet season made it impossible for her to start a fire, and the damp conditions inhibited the growth of fruit-bearing trees. Aware of the potential toxicity of many jungle plants, Juliane exercised caution and refrained from touching unfamiliar vegetation.

On the fourth day of her journey, Juliane's senses heightened as the call of king vultures echoed through the rainforest. Knowing these opportunistic scavengers congregated at carcasses, Juliane followed their ominous calls, leading her to a chilling discovery. Three passengers, still strapped to their seats, had crashed headfirst into the ground with such a force of impact that they were buried three feet with their legs protruding upright.

Despite the shock of this horrendous scene, Juliane examined the woman among them, checking her toes to ensure it was not her mother. The presence of polished nails provided a moment of relief, as her mother never used nail polish. She kept hope that her mother had somehow survived the crash as she had.

Sunburned, starving, and weakened by her arduous journey, Juliane faced a particularly poignant moment of despair by the tenth day of her trek through the Amazon Rainforest. The relentless elements took a heavy toll on her, with ice-cold raindrops drenching her thin summer dress and the wind chilling her to the core. On those bleak nights, seeking shelter under a tree or in a bush, Juliane grappled with the profound sense that she was alone and abandoned.

However, just when she was on the brink of giving up, a glimmer of hope appeared around a bend in the river — a small hut with a palm-leaf roof. This unexpected sight provided a ray of salvation for Juliane.

Inside the small hut, Juliane discovered a can of petrol, a valuable resource in her dire situation. She also realized that her shoulder wound had become infected with maggots. Drawing on her father's knowledge, she decided to use the petrol to address the issue, a method he had employed for a family pet.

She poured the petrol over the wound, enduring intense pain as the maggots attempted to burrow deeper. Undeterred, she took matters into her own hands, removing 30 maggots and feeling relief and pride in her resourcefulness. Satisfied with her efforts, she chose to spend the night in the hut, her first real shelter in the entire ordeal.

———◆———

THE FOLLOWING DAY DELIVERED a surprising and pleasant turn of events. As Juliane awoke to men's voices, she hurriedly emerged from the hut. She saw local Peruvian fishermen, who were initially terrified by the sight of the skinny, dirty, blonde girl, as they mistook her for a mythical water goddess — a figure from local legend described as a hybrid of a water dolphin and a blonde, white-skinned woman.

After enduring 11 harrowing days alone in the jungle, Juliane Koepcke was finally rescued.

Following her rescue and treatment for her injuries, she was reunited with her father. It was then she discovered the heartbreaking news that her mother had initially survived the fall from the sky but then soon succumbed to her injuries.

In the aftermath of the tragedy, Juliane played a crucial role in assisting authorities in locating the wreckage of the plane and the bodies of the victims. Over several days, efforts were made to find and identify the victims. Tragically, 91 people lost their lives in the disaster, including six of the crew.

Subsequently, Juliane relocated to Germany, her parents' native country.

———— ◆ ————

OVER THE YEARS, JULIANE grappled with the perplexing question of why she was the sole survivor of LANSA Flight 508 while 91 other people, including her mother, all perished in the crash. Compounding her survivor's guilt (as some psychologists refer to her unsettled questions), it is believed that 14 people initially survived the impact but were not well enough to navigate their way out of the jungle as Juliane had.

Survival experts have analyzed the remarkable circumstances that contributed to her survival following the harrowing plane crash. According to their insights, one key factor was her seat placement — she occupied the window seat, harnessed into a row of three seats. Aircraft safety experts speculate that this configuration acted like a makeshift parachute, slowing down her descent and potentially mitigating the impact upon landfall.

Moreover, Koepcke's descent through a thunderstorm may have contributed to her survival. The storm's updraft could have further slowed her fall, adding an unexpected yet beneficial element to the chain of events. The thick foliage at her landing site could have also served as a natural cushion, reducing the severity of the impact.

The official cause of the crash was listed as an intentional decision by the airline to fly the plane into hazardous weather conditions. Juliane later discovered that the aircraft was constructed entirely from spare parts salvaged from other planes.

Following the traumatic event, Juliane faced numerous challenges in her life. She became a subject of media attention, and her story was not always portrayed sensitively. The ordeal left her with a profound fear of flying, and she experienced recurring nightmares for years.

Despite the difficulties, Juliane persevered. In 1980, she began studying biology at the University of Kiel in Germany and eventually earned her doctorate. She returned to Peru to conduct research in mammalogy. She married and took the name Juliane Diller as she moved forward with her new life with her husband, Erich.

Her story became better known to the world with a Werner Herzog-directed documentary entitled *Wings of Hope*. Herzog, who was initially scheduled to be on that same LANSA Flight 508 but changed his plans at the last minute, held a longstanding interest in Juliane's experience due to his connection to the flight. The documentary featured Juliane returning to the Amazon and revisiting the site of the crash for the very first time.

During the documentary, Juliane, accompanied by Herzog and her husband, occupied the seat with the same number (19F) she had been in during the crash years earlier. *Wings of Hope* provided a unique perspective on Juliane's journey and the impact of the most traumatic event of her life.

Juliane Koepcke's survival in the face of such overwhelming odds has placed her in a unique and small club of individuals who have defied extraordinary circumstances. The mystery surrounding her survival remains a compelling aspect of her astonishing story.

Our next chapter introduces us to a family's incredible journey of survival after their yacht was shipwrecked, offering another unique perspective on resilience and ingenuity in the cold hands of the vast and unpredictable sea.

5

ODYSSEY IN THE OCEAN

Pacific Ocean off the Galápagos Islands, 1971

The Robertson family's real-life adventure, more thrilling and challenging than any fictional tale, unfolded in the vast expanse of the Pacific Ocean during the 1970s. The family, led by retired merchant navy officer Dougal Robertson, embarked on a global voyage aboard their 43-foot wooden schooner, Lucette. Dougal Robertson sought to provide his children with a unique education in the "university of life."

The family included Dougal's wife Lyn, 18-year-old son Douglas, 17-year-old daughter Anne, and nine-year-old twin sons Neil and Sandy. Leaving behind their dairy farm in Meerbrook, England, the Robertsons set sail from Falmouth, Cornwall, on January 27, 1971. Little did they know that their journey would soon become an extraordinary tale of survival against the elements.

The family's lack of extensive planning and practice for the journey became evident as they faced a life-altering event in the Pacific. A school of killer whales surrounded and attacked their boat, forcing the Robertsons into a desperate struggle for survival in a dinghy for over a month. The ordeal included critical matters of finding food and potable water while being exposed to the harsh conditions of the open sea.

After enduring unimaginable difficulties, the family's story took an unexpected turn when they were rescued by a Japanese fishing boat. The global headlines that followed brought attention to the strong resilience and incredible survival of the Robertson family. Years later, Douglas would recall what happened when they were adrift at sea.

---◆---

FEW PLACES WILL MAKE you feel more hopeless than being lost at sea.

The vast and seemingly endless expanses of water, unpredictable and potentially stormy weather conditions, lack of access to clean drinking water despite having water right in front of you the entire time, and nonstop isolation with no land in sight can very quickly make any person who is physically stuck out on the ocean also mentally stuck in despair.

The open sea presents a stark contrast to solid ground. Still, it's no less forgiving than the icy wastelands of Antarctica, the vast deserts of the Sahara, or the dense jungles of the Amazon Rainforest. The absence of visual landmarks can lead to disorientation and make navigation even more challenging than on land alone.

Unpredictable and extreme weather conditions are a constant threat on the open sea. Storms with high winds, rough seas, and towering waves can appear suddenly and without warning, testing the resilience of both vessels and individuals. Countless lives have been lost at sea when people found their vessels turned over as they plunged into the depths of the ocean, unable to resurface.

Isolation poses a unique psychological challenge. The absence of immediate access to land and other vessels can induce feelings of loneliness and isolation, affecting mental well-being during extended periods at sea. This is why there are countless stories of people adrift at sea who became 'friends' with inanimate objects so that they could have 'someone' to talk to. (This fact was famously reflected in the 2000 film *Cast Away*, where Tom Hanks's character makes friends with a volleyball he names 'Wilson.')

Securing food sources in the ocean requires knowledge of fishing or provisions. Maintaining adequate supplies for the duration of the journey is essential for prolonged survival. Without supplies, food will be limited to fish you can catch or any birds you can capture if they land on your boat to rest.

Seafarers must also contend with potential encounters with marine life, ranging from curious dolphins to potentially dangerous sharks. Swimming in the water, apart from your raft or boat, is one of the most dangerous things you can do.

The isolation of the open sea requires people to be resourceful in constructing makeshift shelters and water desalination. It can be very easy for disorientation and sunburn to set in from constant exposure to the burning sun. Desalination can be used to convert saltwater to freshwater to make it safe to drink, but only if the proper equipment is on hand. Most people who find themselves lost at sea don't have the necessary equipment.

For that reason, many people who have been adrift at sea for extended periods have suffered emotional crises and/or mental breakdowns.

Nonetheless, surviving on the open sea is possible, even for extended periods. The Robertson family's story proves this.

---◆---

THE ROBERTSON FAMILY EMBARKED on their ambitious journey with boundless enthusiasm, living the dream as they set sail across the Atlantic. The family patriarch, Dougal, was exuberant at the helm. Douglas would recall that his father always embodied the thrill of adventure with spirited shouts of "Yee-haa!" Yet, the unpredictable nature of the open sea soon revealed the challenges that lay ahead.

As they sailed across the Atlantic and made stops at various Caribbean ports during the next 17 months, the family encountered the realities of life at sea. The initial excitement gave way to the acknowledgment that their journey would not be a mere paddling across the pond. Battling cold, wet spray and waves breaking across the bow, the Robertsons began to comprehend the unpredictable nature of the ocean.

The family's lack of sailing experience added a layer of complexity to their ill-fated adventure. From the beginning, the Robertsons encountered the unforgiving nature of the sea, confronting a forceful gale in the Bay of Biscay during their initial sail from Falmouth. The harsh conditions and lack of sailing expertise led to a perilous situation, forcing the family to confront the realities of their maritime journey.

A pivotal moment arrived while navigating the Pacific Ocean near the Galapagos Islands, 17 months into their global voyage. The *Lucette* was struck by a pod of killer whales, suddenly plunging the family into a perilous situation. The impact shook the entire boat, and the ominous sounds of cracking wood echoed through the air, reminiscent of a tree trunk being snapped in two.

Douglas vividly recalled the heart-stopping encounter, stating, "I heard this splashing noise behind me, and there were three killer whales following the boat."

Despite the belief by some that even wild killer whales generally pose no threat to humans, the gravity of the situation struck fear into the heart of the then-teenager. The family (accompanied by one Robin Williams, a student hitchhiker they had picked up earlier) tried to patch up the boat, but it was useless. The water was flooding in faster than they could pour it out.

In the aftermath of the killer whale attack on their boat, the Robertson family found themselves facing a dire situation. They swiftly decided to abandon the sinking vessel, jumping overboard into the vast expanse of the Pacific Ocean. The family clung to the liferaft and the dinghy, named *Ednamair*, salvaging what supplies they could in a race against time.

This fateful encounter with the whales marked the most significant turning point in the Robertson family's adventure as they grappled with the harsh realities of the sea on a small raft.

Cut off from the conveniences of their sunken vessel, most of their supplies and provisions with it, the Robertsons were forced to explore alternative sources of sustenance in their battle for survival.

———◆———

THE ROBERTSON FAMILY FOUND themselves resorting to unconventional means to stave off hunger and dehydration during their ordeal in the Pacific Ocean. With their meager supplies dwindling rapidly, Douglas recounted the family's resourcefulness in securing sustenance.

In a stroke of unexpected fortune, a flying fish and a 35-lb. dorado fish leaped into their boats, providing some initial food—raw fish for breakfast. However, the hard reality of their situation pushed them to take more proactive measures. They tied the raft and dinghy together and underwent a challenging quest to hunt for turtles.

Their first attempt was met with challenges, as a passing turtle eluded them despite being struck on its head with an oar. Undeterred, the family developed a more strategic approach. They were able to successfully lift the next turtle out of the water and into the raft. Learning from their experiences, they adapted their methods by tying the subsequent turtles to avoid the chaotic thrashing that occurred when they brought them aboard.

By the third encounter, armed with a kitchen knife, they would quickly kill the turtle. The turtles they captured provided them with a vital source of sustenance.

In the dire circumstances of their survival at sea, the Robertson family navigated the thin line between desperation and resourcefulness. Years later, Douglas shared an insightful revelation that played a crucial role in their unconventional survival tactics.

Inspired by a passage he had read in the novel *South by Java Head*, Douglas proposed the idea to the rest of the family of drinking turtle blood as a potential source of hydration. Intrigued by the prospect, Dougal decided to give it a try on one of the turtles they had captured and killed. To their surprise, it proved a viable solution, offering a much-needed source of liquid sustenance.

In addition to drinking turtle blood, the family employed more measures to make the most of their limited resources. They carefully dried the turtle meat along the boat's sides under the sun, creating a preserved food source that became a critical component of their diet. Their reliance on survival instincts was pivotal in discerning which parts of the captured creatures were safe to consume.

———— ◆ ————

THE ROBERTSON FAMILY'S STRUGGLE for survival unfolded over the next five and a half weeks as they faced relentless challenges. The inflatable raft began showing signs of wear and tear. Holes emerged, and the family was forced to continually pour out the water that seeped in.

Life in the dinghy brought its own set of hardships. The family endured cramped conditions, coping with fierce storms, drought, and the grim realities of hunger, thirst, and exposure. Rainwater became a precious resource, and they collected it diligently. Fishing and constant water bailing were essential tasks as they eked out their meager provisions in a battle against the elements.

To satiate their hunger, the family set up a makeshift fishing line. Yet, their efforts were thwarted by cunning sharks that managed to eat any fish they caught. Despite these setbacks, the family continued to adapt and make the most of the limited resources available on the open sea.

As the days passed and problems mounted, the Robertson family's resilience was tested to its limits. On Day 15, Dougal, determined to salvage the dinghy that had broken free from the raft, bravely dove into the water. Despite facing exhaustion and the lurking threat of sharks, he summoned the strength to retrieve the vital craft. This courageous act underscored the family's determination to survive against all odds.

Facing the bleak reality of limited drinking water, Lyn proposed a creative solution: using the water from the bottom of the dinghy for enemas. While the water was too contaminated for consumption, Lyn's ingenuity sought to utilize it to keep their bodies hydrated. Taking charge,

Douglas crafted makeshift equipment for the enemas. In a testament to the dire circumstances, everyone except Robin agreed to adopt this unconventional method to maintain hydration amid their struggle for survival.

On Day 17, the raft's condition deteriorated to the point where it was no longer viable. Forced to abandon the raft, they salvaged essential items, including flotation pieces to be attached to the bow of the dinghy and the canopy to provide some semblance of shelter.

July 4, Day 20, marked a rather sweet occasion: Lyn's birthday. Amid their dire circumstances, the family gathered to sing "Happy Birthday" and partake in a modest feast comprising fresh turtle meat, dried turtle meat, and dried dorado fish meat. Despite the scarcity of resources, they managed to create a semblance of celebration, savoring the moment with water as their only beverage.

As their ordeal extended into the 21st day in the dinghy, the toll on their bodies became evident. Sores and cramps plagued them due to the lack of movement and the unforgiving conditions. Despite this, the family pressed on, knowing the likelihood of anyone searching for them was slim. Their isolation meant that nobody was aware of their plight, adding to the gravity of their predicament.

By Day 27, having weathered numerous harrowing storms, the family resorted to using turtle oil extracted from the fat for enemas to soothe their damaged skin. Each passing day tested their endurance, but their determination to survive persisted.

As more days unfolded, the Robertson family's struggle for survival took additional unexpected turns. On Day 29, Dougal's encounter with a five-foot Mako shark added a dramatic twist. Despite the danger, he successfully hauled the shark on board, ultimately decapitating it with the kitchen knife. The severed head, however, inflicted a wound on Dougal's hand, leaving a mark that would serve as a unique souvenir.

By Day 36, the toll of their journey manifested in their worn-out clothing. Lyn, displaying remarkable resourcefulness, washed and mended their tattered garments with the limited supplies from her sewing kit — a small yet invaluable asset that played a crucial role in their survival.

The physical toll was particularly evident in the younger members of the family. Neil's emaciated condition and Sandy's persistent cough (possibly indicating pneumonia) underscored the severity of their predicament without access to professional medical care. Yet, despite the physical challenges and their dwindling resources, the Robertson family kept going, driven by an unwavering will to endure.

———— ◆ ————

ON JULY 23, 1972, their distress flare caught the crew's attention aboard the Japanese fishing trawler, the Toka Maru II, en route to the Panama Canal. The sight that greeted the Japanese sailors was nothing short of extraordinary. After enduring 38 days of harrowing survival at sea, the Robertson family's seabound ordeal ended.

The Robertsons, along with student Robin Williams, were found in their dinghy *Ednamair*, having traversed more than 750 miles by raft and dinghy. When they were rescued, they still had approximately 290 miles left to reach land. The family's resilience and tenacity astounded the Japanese rescuers, who couldn't believe the remarkable tale of survival they had stumbled upon.

Following their rescue, Robin flew back to England, while the Robertson family returned by ship, the MV Port Auckland. The family's daughter, Anne, awaited their return, and soon, the entire Robertson family was reunited, marking the end of an extraordinary chapter in their lives.

Douglas later reflected on the incredible twist of fate. Dougal had been a survivor of a sinking by the Japanese in Ceylon (now Sri Lanka) in 1942 during World War II, only now to be rescued by Japanese sailors in 1971. Douglas couldn't help but remark on the irony.

Douglas also revealed that the family had made a pact on the very first day of their shipwreck: they vowed not to resort to the desperate measures of cannibalism, a chilling tradition known among sailors as the "custom of the sea." In this tradition, survivors of shipwrecks might draw straws, and the unfortunate one with the short straw would become sustenance for the others upon his demise.

Rejecting this gruesome option, the Robertsons collectively committed to face whatever fate awaited them together. Douglas emphasized that even though Robin was not a blood relative, they assured him that he was considered part of their family and that they all would stand united.

———◆———

THE ROBERTSON FAMILY'S EXTRAORDINARY saga, recounted in Dougal Robertson's book *Survive the Savage Sea*, not only became a gripping written tale of survival but also inspired a film.

Using the proceeds from the book, Dougal purchased another boat and chose to live in the Mediterranean. Meanwhile, his wife Lyn returned to farming. Douglas followed a different path, joining the Navy and then becoming an accountant. The family's resilience and ability to find positivity in adversity are evident in their diverse pursuits after their ordeal at sea.

In 2008, the Robertson family donated the *Ednamair* to the National Maritime Museum in Falmouth, Cornwall. Reflecting on the entire experience, Douglas expressed no regrets. Despite the darkest hours they'd endured, he claimed a unique quality of life at sea, with the essence of survival and the profound reward of witnessing each new sunset and sunrise. The journey, challenging as it was, instilled in the entire family a connection with the natural world's instinct for survival, where living another day becomes the ultimate goal.

Douglas also contends that the true story of the *Lucette* remains a concealed secret. He softly criticizes his father's book for only covering the days after the shipwreck, presenting a dry and academic account derived from the voyage log. Even the film adaptation took creative liberties, deviating from the actual events—for instance, the movie depicts the family sailing from Australia, not England.

In an attempt to reveal the comprehensive story, Douglas wrote his own book in 2005, titled *The Last Voyage of the Lucette*. However, the book didn't gain much attention due to a personal tragedy that overshadowed its publication. At the time when Douglas should have been promoting his book, he found himself at his son Joshua's bedside in intensive care. Joshua had experienced a near-fatal motorbike accident in Australia, diverting the family's focus away from the recounting of the Robertson saga.

Douglas's book revealed that once the family was on the raft, Douglas and his father devised a plan that proved crucial to their survival. Instead of aiming for land, they set a course for water, explicitly sailing 400 miles north to the Doldrums.

Life on the raft was harsh, Douglas recalled. The raft had sustained damage during launch, which worsened over time, leaving them sitting with water up to their chests. Saltwater sores afflicted their bodies, and the stifling heat leached the energy from them. The family took turns sitting on the relatively dry thwart (seat), with Lyn often sacrificing her turn for the comfort of others. Sleep was elusive due to the constant fear of drowning in their sleep, especially for the young twins.

Conversely, the Ednamair was dry but fragile. The constant threat of being swamped by waves kept them on edge. On the 23rd day, heavy rain almost caused the dinghy to sink, and Dougal considered giving up before rallying the family to empty the small craft of water.

Their resilience was fueled by sheer determination, perseverance, and an unconventional source of sustenance—turtle blood. Drinking it quickly was imperative to prevent it from congealing, and its unpleasant after-taste made it difficult to swallow.

Lyn, drawing on her nursing background, applied turtle oil to their saltwater boils and attempted to keep them hydrated by using makeshift enema tubes crafted from a ladder's rungs. She knew the water at the dinghy's bottom, a concoction of rainwater, blood, and turtle offal, was poisonous if ingested orally. By introducing it rectally, they avoided the harmful effects.

Ultimately, the Robertson family's survival at sea showcased a remark-able array of skills and strategies. Their resourcefulness was evident in collecting rainwater during drought and in their ability to catch fish, turtles, and other sea creatures for sustenance. Their decision to aim for water instead of land reflected a keen sense of adaptation to their conditions.

For individuals facing similar challenges at sea, the key takeaways include prioritizing water and food sources, having emergency supplies such as life rafts and medical kits, acquiring basic navigation skills, staying calm, and fostering unity within a group. The Robertsons' continuous adapt-ability, whether in repairing a leaking raft or adjusting fishing strategies, underscores the importance of flexibility in navigating unpredictable scenarios.

Survival at sea demands practical skills, adaptability, and mental re-silience. It emphasizes the need for improvisation and sound deci-sion-making in open-water survival scenarios.

———— ◆ ————

DESPITE HIS FATHER'S GUILT about the trip, Douglas believes that his parents never ceased to love each other. Dougal passed away from cancer at the age of 67, with Lyn by his side to care for him during the last three years of his life. Lyn, at the age of 75, also succumbed to cancer. Douglas later had his own family with five children.

Reflecting on his father's remorse for getting his family into the situation, Douglas highlights the family's accomplishment, reassuring Dougal that they survived and thrived through the experience.

"Life is an adventure, and the things we learned here apply to everyone else's normal life," Douglas said. "Never give up, deal with each problem as it comes, and have hope; as long as there's life, there's hope, and it did turn out alright in the end. Nobody died and we got home."

Despite the hardships, the Robertson family's story is a testament to resilience, unity, and the triumph of the human spirit. Our next story takes us from the ocean's vastness to some of the highest mountain peaks in the world in the Peruvian Andes.

6

TRIUMPH IN THE ANDES

Peruvian Andes Mountains, 1985

In 1985, renowned British mountaineer Joe Simpson embarked on his most perilous adventure yet into South America with his climbing partner Simon Yates. Their mission was to conquer the daunting Siula Grande in the Andes Mountains of Peru. Little did they know that this expedition would turn into a harrowing tale of survival that would test the limits of their endurance, mental resilience, and even their will to live.

Siula Grande, proudly standing tall at 20,800+ feet, poses a formidable challenge to even the most experienced climbers. Simpson and Yates were driven by a shared passion for conquering challenging mountain climbs. They each believed that successfully climbing Siula Grande would be one of their most remarkable feats in high-altitude mountaineering.

The duo also knew about treacherous terrain and would be up against chilling winds and icy slopes. But the camaraderie that grew between Simpson and Yates during the climb was palpable, and despite meeting just before the climb, they knew they had to trust each other fully for what was to come. What they didn't anticipate was that their journey up the jagged mountain slopes of Siula Grande would take an abrupt turn on their way back down, leading to an epic struggle for survival against the unforgiving forces of nature.

———————◆———————

SURVIVING IN THE ANDES Mountains is a formidable challenge due to the region's extreme conditions and diverse landscapes. The high elevations, with peaks exceeding 20,000 feet, expose individuals to the risks of acute mountain sickness and high-altitude cerebral edema, which are exacerbated by the lower oxygen levels at higher altitudes.

The unpredictable weather in the Andes further complicates survival efforts. Rapid temperature changes, intense sunlight, and sudden snow or rain storms are common, posing threats of hypothermia, frostbite, and dehydration. Traveling through the mountains involves treacherous terrain, including steep slopes, glaciers, and deep valleys. The isolation from the rugged landscape makes it challenging to receive timely assistance, highlighting the importance of self-sufficiency.

Limited vegetation and resources add to the challenge. The harsh climates and high altitudes restrict the types of plant life that can thrive, impacting both human and animal food sources. Access to clean water is also a concern, requiring careful planning and resourcefulness. The diverse terrain of the Andes, from rocky peaks to deep gorges, poses risks of avalanches, landslides, and rockfalls, requiring specialized skills and equipment to make your way out.

———◆———

JOE SIMPSON WAS BORN on August 13, 1960, in Kuala Lumpur, Malaysia. He developed a passion for climbing from an early age, spurred by his first reading of the 1938 book *The White Spider,* which detailed the first known successful ascent of the Eiger mountain in Switzerland. Simpson carried this passion into adulthood and ascended several challenging peaks worldwide before his attempt at Siula Grande. Simon Yates was born on August 29, 1963, and also became an avid mountain climber.

The two not only wanted to climb Siula Grande together but also wanted to climb it from a pathway that had never been completed before. Siula Grande is located in the harsh Huayhuash mountain range of the Peruvian Andes. The west face of Siula Grande, the route Simpson and Yates chose, required technical climbing, including steep ice and daunting rock faces. The route provided a way for the climbers to reach the summit successfully, but they would face life-threatening difficulties during their descent, as Simpson and Yates would soon discover.

The climb up the mountain went largely according to plan. Atop the mountain, the two men could gaze upon the expansive beauty of the

Andes. Yet, as any seasoned mountaineer knows, the descent often presents challenges that rival, if not exceed, the ascent. This was especially true for the Siula Grande. Simpson and Yates had to climb nearly vertical rock faces during their ascent, which would prove even more challenging during their descent.

The fateful moment arrived when Yates plunged through a deceptive cornice, hanging precariously over the precipice by a rope connected to Simpson. In this harrowing instance, the strength of the rope connecting them kept Yates from plunging to his death as Simpson hoisted him back up. Yates later recalled that the cornice led to an abyss that he estimated to be more than four thousand feet deep.

The incident shook the two, and as the weather grew more severe, they decided to take a break and seek refuge in a snow hole, where they dug in for a freezing night. By this point, the two faced depleting supplies and consumed the last remnants of their food while melting snow for hydration with their portable heater.

But things only got worse the next day.

While continuing their descent the following afternoon, Simpson fell from an ice cliff and landed on his leg at an awkward angle, breaking his tibia and causing the bone to protrude deep into his knee joint. As ominous weather encroached and daylight waned, the two men knew they needed to descend rapidly to the glacier, a daunting 3,000 feet below, before nature unleashed its ice-filled fury upon them. The descent was now a race against time.

Since Simpson could no longer walk, the men were forced to employ a different strategy to get down the mountain. Joining their two 150-foot ropes to create a single 300-foot lifeline, Yates could control Simpson's descent using a belay plate.

The proceeding descent unfolded in three stages for each rope length. Negotiating the conjoined ropes presented a distinct challenge, demanding a strategic approach, and the absence of belay points on the steep open snow and ice slope forced the men to improvise. They could excavate a shallow cavity, in essence fashioning a seat where Yates could anchor himself and absorb the strain of Simpson's weight on the rope to maintain control over the descent.

Yates began to lower Simpson 150 feet until the knot in the rope reached the belay plate since the knot could not fit through. Trying to hold himself to the side of the mountain while tied to the rope, Simpson relieved the tension for Yates by standing on his uninjured leg.

Yates then deftly unclipped the rope, rethreaded it through the lowering device with the knot on the opposite side, and continued the descent for an additional 150 feet. The duo repeated this intricate dance of lowering and downclimbing, constructing makeshift stances along the way.

The approach proved effective, as Yates masterfully lowered Simpson by approximately 3,000 feet. After making good progress for several hours, the climbers only had one more lowering before they could get Simpson to the glacier. They thought things couldn't get any worse after Simpson's severe leg injury, but they were soon in for a rude awakening.

DARK CLOUDS BREWED OVERHEAD and the wind picked up in the last hour of the day. Yates, positioned higher up the mountain, was no longer able to see or hear Simpson, rendering him unable to gauge his precarious position fully. He could only discern the immense strain on the rope, signaling that Simpson dangled freely as his entire weight was still suspended.

Little did he know that Simpson was now being lowered over the edge of a cliff to the point that he was hanging freely over the side rather than having his hands and feet on the mountainside.

Simpson was now solely reliant on the tensioned rope. If the rope broke, he would fall to his death. The tension in the rope was his only way of communicating with Yates. They only had around a hundred more feet to go, and it was now that nature seemed to conspire against them.

The howling winds grew stronger. Simpson desperately attempted to climb the mountain using Prusik loops, but it was complicated. His hands were frostbitten, and he accidentally dropped one of the loops he needed to ascend.

The men were now in grave danger. Simpson could no longer climb up the rope, Yates could no longer pull him back up, and they could not communicate. Furthermore, the cliff was too high, and the rope was too short, so Yates could not continue lowering Simpson even if he wanted to.

The two men remained in this position for over 90 minutes, with Simpson's weight forcing Yates downhill in small steps. Yates would fall a few feet and catch his footing, only to fall and catch his footing again.

Yates's heart raced as he realized that by holding onto the rope with Simpson, he would die...and likely take Simpson with him. If he cut the rope, he could save his own life but possibly kill Simpson.

Yates was now forced to make one of the most critical decisions of his life. He could either cut the rope and save his own life and hope that Simpson was far enough down the cliff that his fall would be negligible, or not cut the rope and most likely ensure death for both of them.

Drawing his knife, Yates cut the rope.

Simpson plummeted down the cliff and fell into a crevasse.

———◆———

BATTERED BY THE ELEMENTS and enduring exhaustion, hypothermia, and frostbite, Yates sought refuge in a snow cave as the storm intensified. He spent the whole night waiting out the storm, unsure of what had happened to Simpson. He was wrecked with grief at the strong possibility that his friend was dead.

The following morning, as weather conditions cleared, Yates continued his precarious descent down the mountainside. When he reached the glacier, he surveyed the landscape and identified the position where Simpson had perilously hung. Looking over, he could not see signs of Simpson, but he saw the crevasse.

Yates realized the gravity of the situation, comprehending that Simpson might have fallen into the crevasse when the rope was severed. Approaching the edge, he called out to Simpson but received no response. Concluding that Simpson was killed by the fall, Yates continued the descent alone.

In reality, despite the harrowing fall of more than 200 feet into the crevasse, Simpson had miraculously survived. Upon regaining consciousness after his fall, he realized that the rope connecting him to Yates above had been severed. Aware that Yates might presume him dead, Simpson understood that he had to fend for himself.

But his broken leg and the slick ice walls of the crevasse made it impossible for him to climb back up to the crevasse entrance with the minimal equipment he had on hand. Left with no alternative, he dared to abseil deeper into the crevasse, hoping to find another exit.

Simpson crawled through the icy corridor, traversed a snow bridge, and reached a steep snow slope. Determined, he climbed the hill, ultimately returning to the top of the glacier.

As it turned out, a twist of fortune favored both climbers. Yates's previous cut happened to be in the middle of the 300-foot rope, providing each with sufficient length to address their immediate predicaments.

Yates had utilized his portion of the rope to abseil safely to the glacier.

Meanwhile, Simpson employed his rope to navigate to a point where he could commence his ascent.

After reaching the glacier, Simpson spent three days crawling and hopping five miles back to their base camp, making sure to carefully avoid falling into more crevasses.

Exhausted and delirious, Simpson reached the base camp only a few hours before Yates and Richard Hawking, the third group member who was a non-climber, were set to depart. He was barely alive and had lost over a third of his body weight in the ordeal, but he had made it back.

When Yates saw that Simpson had made it back alive, he was amazed. He ran over to his friend and the two embraced.

———◆———

THE DECISION YATES HAD to make is hopefully one that you nor I will ever have to. After cutting the rope, Yates spent the entire rest of the descent believing that Simpson was dead. The decision he made itself was a massive gamble, but at the end of the day, it was the decision that ultimately saved him. Had Yates not cut the rope, he would have indeed fallen over the edge of the cliff too, and been killed.

Simpson's part of the ordeal exemplifies the importance of perseverance when confronted with seemingly insurmountable odds. His survival of the fall into the crevasse after Yates cut the rope was perhaps by the grace of God alone. Afterward, however, Simpson's struggle to make it out was nothing short of extraordinary.

Despite facing extreme conditions, severe injury, and isolation, Simpson demonstrated an unwavering determination to survive. He recalled that the fact he was only 25 years old was what kept him going. He believed that he had so much to do in his life and that he couldn't afford to die young.

This psychological strength is evident throughout the ordeal. From critical decision-making on the mountain to enduring isolation and the physical and mental toll of the journey back, he displayed remarkable strength of mind. Their ability to stoically maintain composure, make rational choices, and endure psychological tests, including pain, is a testament to the importance of mental resilience in survival situations.

The story of Joe Simpson and Simon Yates underscores the power of the human will to endure and overcome extreme circumstances, showcasing an innate instinct for survival that people have, even in the most adverse conditions.

The two men recounted their story in a 1988 memoir called *Touching the Void*, which was also made into an acclaimed 2003 documentary and a 2018 stage adaptation. The book sold over a million copies and helped make the general public aware of the dangers of mountain climbing, which requires not only natural skill for ascending and descending mountainsides but also an extraordinary amount of courage.

As Simpson recalled later, "To be a serious climber, you have to be a little unhinged."

From the cold, high altitudes of the Peruvian Andes, we now return to the ocean with the story of Salvador Alvarenga, who spent no less than 438 days adrift at sea.

438 Days Adrift in the Pacific

Pacific Ocean, 2014

At 33, José Salvador Alvarenga was a seasoned shark fisherman with a long history of braving the Pacific Ocean off the coast of Mexico.

Typically, he embarked on two-to-three-day fishing expeditions with a companion on a small boat, capturing sharks and returning to shore to sell his catch for 50 cents a pound. However, fate took an unexpected turn on a November day in 2012 when Alvarenga's regular fishing partner was unavailable for that particular date.

In a spur-of-the-moment decision, he enlisted the help of Ezequiel Cordoba, a 22-year-old novice with limited seafaring experience who usually worked as a day laborer on the beach.

What Alvarenga and Ezequiel didn't anticipate was the extraordinary adventure of survival that awaited them when they ventured out into the ocean that day. What started as a routine fishing trip became a harrowing tale of survival as the two men were adrift at sea for over a year.

———— • ————

ALVARENGA WAS BORN IN El Salvador in 1975. He was the son of a flour mill and store owner in their small hometown. He had a daughter who grew up alongside his parents in their town, as well as several brothers who lived in the United States. In 2002, he left El Salvador for Mexico, where he pursued a career as a fisherman for four years. At the point of his rescue, Alvarenga had lost contact with his family for eight years.

Alvarenga's fishing boat was a 24-foot fiberglass skiff with a small motor. Onboard, he and Ezequiel carried an array of fishing tools, a portable electronic radio, and a substantial icebox to store their catch. The journey initially promised a bountiful harvest, with Alvarenga's optimism seemingly justified as they quickly amassed over a thousand pounds of fish, nearly overwhelming their icebox.

Thus far, everything was going according to plan, and Ezequiel had proved himself to be a worthy fisherman.

Then disaster struck.

Just a few hours into their journey, Alvarenga and Cordoba were confronted by a relentless storm that persisted for five days. While battling the elements, they attempted to navigate the boat back toward the elusive shore, but to no avail. The storm damaged the motor and wreaked havoc on most of their portable electronics.

Struggling against the tempest, Alvarenga and Cordoba faced the heartbreaking decision to dump nearly all of their freshly caught fish overboard, sacrificing their hard-earned bounty to regain control of the vessel in the treacherous weather conditions. When the boat continued to be in danger of falling under the high waves, the men also threw out their water supply to lighten the boat up further so it could stay afloat.

Alvarenga was willing to risk throwing the water overboard because he believed he could call or signal for help. Using a two-way radio, he made a distress call to his boss, Rodriguez, before the device succumbed to its dying battery. To drink, the duo relied on the rainwater that generously poured from the sky and the limited food provisions they had brought along.

Though relentless in its fury at first, the storm eventually subsided, allowing the men a brief respite to assess the extensive damage wrought upon their vessel by nature's unrelenting forces.

Now utterly devoid of sails, oars, anchors, running lights, and any means of contacting the shore, José and Ezequiel were at the mercy of the ocean's whims.

They were stranded without a functioning radio, a functional motor, or ample provisions. Holding onto the hope that Alvarenga's distress call to Rodriguez would trigger a rescue mission, they began the arduous process of survival amid the vast expanse of the sea. Despite Cordoba's limited usefulness due to his inexperience as a fisherman, Alvarenga's extensive fishing experience proved invaluable as he resorted to catching fish, turtles, jellyfish, and seabirds with his bare hands.

Rainwater collection became a sporadic source of hydration. Still, they sustained themselves more often than not with a mixture of their own urine and turtle blood, adapting to the unforgiving conditions in their fight for survival.

Meanwhile, Rodriguez's search party proved futile in finding any trace of the missing men, and the search was abandoned after two days due to poor visibility.

Alvarenga and Cordoba were stranded at sea, and no one was searching for them.

———— ♦ ————

As the days stretched into weeks and the weeks morphed into months, José and Ezequiel resigned themselves to the grim reality of their situation. Hope for rescue dwindled, and their survival depended on the slim chance of being spotted by passing planes or drifting into a random shipping lane.

However, lacking any means of navigation, the prospect of being rescued seemed increasingly remote.

During the initial month, they feasted on sea turtles, which were sometimes abundant. They consumed the blood in multiple glasses before they consumed the meat.

Commonly accompanying turtles were small sharks, usually under two or three feet. Alvarenga, taking advantage of their size, would wait until the sharks approached the boat and then seize them by the back fin. The shark livers became a valuable addition to their diet, as they are rich in oils and nutrition.

Alvarenga also ingeniously utilized a stick to create a makeshift perch, luring birds to 'land.' Initially attentive, the birds relaxed, preening their feathers and dozing off. Alvarenga, lying motionless beneath the stick, swiftly raised his arm, seizing the bird by the leg and pulling it down, breaking a wing. This method, while harsh, ensured that the two men collected a stockpile of 20-30 birds on the boat that couldn't escape.

Alvarenga, drawing upon his experience and familiarity with the sea, found hope in charting the phases of the moon to keep track of time. Having grown up on the water and spending most of his life at sea, he had adapted to a diet primarily composed of seafood and relied on the sun and moon to guide him.

In contrast, Ezequiel faced a greater challenge adjusting to the harsh realities of their situation. Despite Alvarenga's attempts to keep Ezequiel hopeful and teach him how to keep track of time using the sun and the moon, Ezequiel's hope slowly but steadily dwindled.

◆

AROUND SIX TO TEN weeks into their journey, the men attempted to discern if it was Christmas by observing the full moon. Opting for a 'festive' dinner, they decided on two birds each from the ones Alvarenga had caught.

After filleting the birds with a knife and commencing their Christmas feast, Ezequiel began to gag. Bubbles emerged from his mouth, indicating he was being poisoned!

Perplexed, they investigated the bird carcass and discovered a small, poisonous yellow snake in the stomach. Ezequiel has been poisoned due to the bird ingesting the toxic snake.

Alvarenga tried to nurse Ezequiel back to health, but the young man had lost confidence in eating anything. Despite Alvarenga's attempts to feed him small bits of food placed on fish vertebrae made into a toothpick, Ezequiel never overcame his fear of eating food for the rest of his voyage.

Ezequiel found himself on the brink of physical deterioration and mental exhaustion. The toll of their new lives adrift at sea manifested in this deteriorating health, which was further exacerbated by his refusal to eat enough food.

Alvarenga recalled that around the four-month mark, Ezequiel's spirit and his will to live waned, and his illness from the snake poison and subsequent loss of food only became worse. Eventually, he decided to stop eating altogether, passing away from self-imposed starvation. Before he died, Ezequiel made Alvarenga promise not to resort to cannibalism upon his death.

Overwhelmed by grief at his failure to save his companion's life and by the sheer magnitude of his hopeless situation, Alvarenga admitted contemplating suicide for four days, which he later claimed were the most agonizing of the whole ordeal.

Struggling with solitude and grappling with potential insanity, Alvarenga kept Ezequiel's corpse in the boat for six days, engaging in conversations with the lifeless form beside him as if he were still alive. Eventually, battling the fear of losing his sanity, he made the heart-wrenching decision to release Ezequiel's body into the depths of the ocean.

Alvarenga was now totally alone, and he would remain so for several months. He was able to find a new companion, however, when he discovered a unique bird among the others that landed on his boat. Rather than kill it, he decided to make it his companion.

He brought the bird into his shelter and provided it with special meals so it would stay with him. Named Pancho, this bird became the only friend Alvarenga had for the rest of his survival ordeal and helped to alleviate the solitude he faced.

He grew more desperate when his attempts to seek help from numerous transoceanic container ships proved futile, but he tried to sustain his sanity by using the moon to keep track of the days. He continued to use his fishing skills to catch fish and collect rainwater to survive.

———— ♦ ————

ON JANUARY 30, 2014, after enduring 438 days of the relentless trials of the open sea, Alvarenga spotted dry land in the distance. Little did he know it was a remote islet within the Marshall Islands.

Upon spotting the land, the relieved Alvarenga didn't hesitate. He leaped from his boat into the ocean and swam to shore. His determination carried him through the waves despite his weakened state. Upon reaching the shoreline, he chanced upon a modest beach house that was owned by a local couple.

The couple, after providing him with food and bedding and hearing his extraordinary tale, promptly alerted the authorities. The police, initially believing Alvarenga had perished almost a year ago, were astounded to find him not only alive but surprisingly well, given the circumstances.

Alvarenga was reunited with his family, whom he had not seen for eight years. They were overjoyed to see him.

But then the questions started coming in.

Many people began wondering how it was possible that Alvarengo could have survived for that long. He also faced troubles from Ezequiel's family.

Initial skepticism surrounded his account. His robust health contradicted expectations of severe emaciation after spending over a year at sea. Though thin, with unkempt hair and a weathered look on his face that made him look older than he was, the absence of food and fresh water for such an extended period should have led to extreme emaciation...or so doctors hypothesized. The lack of scurvy, at the very least, puzzled medical expectations.

Maritime experts, on the other hand, raised questions about the feasibility of reaching the Marshall Islands without a steering mechanism or navigation system. Sailing from the Mexican coast to the Marshall Islands requires a near-straight line and seems rather impossible.

Furthermore, Alvarenga faced a lawsuit from Ezequiel's family. Their lawsuit asserted that Alvarenga did not dispose of Ezequiel's body at sea but instead resorted to cannibalism, using his remains for sustenance. Alvarenga's attorney vehemently refuted these allegations, and Alvarenga even underwent a lie detector test to substantiate his denial.

Furthermore, various medical professionals highlighted that Alvarenga's maritime diet, primarily composed of bird and sea turtle meat, provided substantial amounts of vitamin C, effectively preventing scurvy. The debate regarding his route was also resolved when a University of Hawaii study demonstrated that ocean currents could have naturally guided him to the island where he ultimately landed.

———◆———

ALVARENGA'S SURVIVAL DURING HIS extended ordeal at sea can be attributed to a combination of remarkable factors. His resourcefulness and creativity played a pivotal role as he adapted to the challenges by employing innovative strategies for catching fish, sharks, and even birds.

Basically, he ensured a sustainable food supply by using his skills. His adaptation to a diverse diet, including turtles, shark liver, and unconventional sea creatures allowed him to extract vital nutrients, so he was not as emaciated as one would expect for someone lost at sea for so long.

Possessing essential sea skills as a seasoned fisherman, Alvarenga's familiarity with the ocean and adept fishing techniques contributed significantly to his survival. His mental resilience was also a key factor, as Alvarenga endured harsh weather conditions, boredom from sitting on the boat for months, and overcoming the loss of his companion.

His faith that a better life awaited him after he returned to civilization also helped sustain him, preventing despair during taxing moments and aiding in his coping with isolation and loss. His connection with the pet bird named Pancho also provided a degree of companionship, alleviating the psychological toll of isolation and loneliness.

In short, Alvarenga's ability to combine practical skills, adaptability, and psychological resilience ultimately led to his survival. When his boat reached the Marshall Islands, he was in excellent condition for someone lost so long at sea.

Next, we move in from the vastness of the ocean to the coastlines of California.

200-FOOT PLUNGE OFF A CALIFORNIA CLIFF

Coastline off Big Sur, California, 2018

Angela Hernandez's harrowing ordeal along California's Central Coast began with a traumatic accident, the details of which were hazy for her.

In 2018, the then 23-year-old from Portland, Oregon, suffered severe injuries, including a fractured collarbone and ribs and the loss of air from one of her lungs. Despite the impact, Angela didn't recall the specifics of the accident, such as hitting her head. Her vivid memories started with regaining consciousness, finding herself trapped in her SUV in the Pacific Ocean.

In a social media post the weekend after the incident, Angela expressed the profound impact of the prior week, describing it as an unparalleled experience in her young life. Her account provides a glimpse into her extraordinary story of survival during those seven days of adversity along the rugged coastal terrain.

⸻

SURVIVING BY THE OCEAN coast under a cliff, where climbing out is not an option, presents challenges that require extraordinary resilience and the ability to use limited resources.

Coastal areas are always prone to tide-related hazards, including high tides and unpredictable waves. It is crucial to monitor the ocean's dynamic behavior and adapt accordingly. While the cliffs offer natural shelter, the confined space underneath poses challenges for securing a camp.

The rugged nature of coastal cliffs further presents safety risks, such as rockfalls and landslides, demanding constant attention and alertness to ensure you won't become a victim.

———◆———

ANGELA'S SURVIVAL STORY UNFOLDED on July 6 as she drove through California's Big Sur area, bound for Southern California. To avoid a small animal on the highway, she drastically swerved, careening off the cliff's edge. Her vehicle crashed some 200 feet below, where the ocean meets a remote and rocky beach.

In her Facebook post recounting the traumatic experience, Angela vividly described waking up trapped in her SUV, surrounded by rising water and grappling with injuries.

She wrote, "The only thing I remember after that was waking up. I was still in my car, and I could feel water rising over my knees. My head hurt, and when I touched it, I found blood on my hands. Every bone in my body hurt." Angela's resourcefulness became crucial for survival as she used a multi-tool to shatter the driver-side window.

Once free and managing to swim to shore, she succumbed to exhaustion and lost consciousness for an unknown duration. When she awoke to her dire circumstances, she faced a landscape of rocks, the vast ocean, and an insurmountable cliff. Her car was partially washed ashore with its roof torn off.

Determined to find help despite her injuries, Angela walked along the desolate fog-covered beach and climbed rocks in search of another person. The rocky and secluded terrain made her nearly invisible to drivers on the highway above. In her quest for rescue, she shouted for help, hoping someone would hear her pleas.

The subsequent days for Angela were undoubtedly a harrowing ordeal. Bereft of shoes and equipped only with tattered socks and jeans reduced to shreds, she continued to navigate the treacherous terrain of sun-baked rocks in her desperate search for assistance. The cliff in front of her, however, was impossible to climb. Sunburned, hungry, and dehydrated, she resorted to resourcefulness for survival.

As the days passed, Angela faced the cruel reality of dehydration. Around the third day, stranded on the beach, she began feeling the effects of thirst. Resourcefully, she discovered a 10-inch radiator hose, which she used to siphon water from a nearby natural spring to quench her thirst and increase her chances of survival.

To treat the sun burns on her face, she walked close to the ocean and applied wet sand to her hair to stay cool during the day. In her social media post, Angela revealed that songs, some she hadn't heard in years, played in her head and served as a source of positivity until her eventual rescue.

———————◆———————

MEANWHILE, LAW ENFORCEMENT HAD been actively searching the Central Coast for Angela. They utilized surveillance footage from a Big Sur gas station and a few cell phone pings—though the region has spotty reception—to narrow down the search to a 60-mile stretch of rugged coastal cliffs between Nacimiento-Ferguson Road and the Carmel Highlands.

The Monterey County Sheriff's Office provided a statement revealing that Angela was last seen on surveillance footage on July 6 driving her white 2011 Jeep down Highway 1. John Thornburg, a public information officer for the sheriff's office, later told *The Washington Post* that the heavy fog from the coast might have hindered first responders' locating her and the wreckage.

Meanwhile, below the road, Angela was enduring an agonizing wait for rescue. She spent her days watching cars traverse the cliffs above, yet no one noticed her. The distance likely muted her desperate calls for help.

In her Facebook post, she vividly expressed her yearning: "I could see cars driving across the cliff and felt like if I could yell just loud enough, that one could hear or see me... That's all it would take to make it back to my family. Just one person noticed me."

Despite the search efforts from law enforcement above, the isolation of the rocky beach concealed Angela from sight, decreasing the likelihood of being rescued. The disconnect between the ongoing search efforts and her undetected presence created a stark contrast, underscoring the difficulty of finding a single person stranded in such rugged terrain.

———— ♦ ————

AFTER A UNIVERSALLY DEMANDING week of traversing the beach, navigating hot rocks, and desperately calling out to distant cars for help, Angela Hernandez's prayers were answered. Chad and Chelsea Moore, hiking along the beach, heard her faint cries for help.

Their initial intention was to collect items that had spilled from Angela's car during the accident. However, as they combed through the rocks, they stumbled upon Angela, hidden and battered. Chad described Angela as appearing worn but happy when they found her. Astonished by the encounter, Chelsea shared their disbelief, realizing that the battered car they had seen earlier belonged to the living survivor before them.

In recounting the moment, Angela expressed her initial disbelief when she spotted the couple. Convinced it was another dream, she screamed for help and rushed towards them. The couple, quick to respond, played a vital role in her rescue.

Chelsea swiftly ran down the beach and up a trail to seek help, while Chad stayed with Angela, providing her with much-needed fresh water. Their prompt and caring actions proved crucial to her rescue and ultimate survival.

Chelsea recounted, "I heard a faint cry for help, and I turned, and we saw

Angela standing on the rocks. She said she woke up that morning and knew it would be a good day, and I think I started crying."

The treacherous terrain posed a significant obstacle for the rescuers. The area lacked suitable trails for Angela to navigate, especially given her injuries. Even for a fit and healthy individual, the rugged landscape would have presented a formidable challenge.

Instead, the rescuers deployed a California Highway Patrol helicopter. Equipped with a stretcher, the helicopter airlifted Angela out of the remote area and transported her to Twin Cities Community Hospital in Templeton.

———◆———

ANGELA LATER SHARED ON social media that doctors revealed she had suffered a brain hemorrhage, fractures to four ribs and her collarbone, a collapsed lung, and ruptured blood vessels in both eyes, among other injuries.

After her incident, Angela recounted, "I feel like I have everything I've ever wanted. I'm sitting here in the hospital, laughing with my sister until she makes broken bones hurt. I've met some of the most beautiful human beings that I think I'll ever meet in my entire life. I've experienced something so unique and terrifying that I can't imagine there isn't a bigger purpose for me in this life. I don't know, you guys, life is incredible."

Angela had indeed survived against all odds, not only by miraculously surviving the crash itself but also by braving the elements and using ingenious methods to remain alive.

In our next and final chapter, we'll dive into the heroic rescue of a trapped Thai youth soccer team, highlighting the power of teamwork in survival situations.

9

TEAMWORK IN THAM LUANG CAVE

Northern Thailand (underground), 2018

If you were trapped in an underground cavern that was flooding with water, what would you do?

In June and July 2018, a junior association football team became trapped in Tham Luang Nang Non, a cave system in the Chiang Rai province of northern Thailand, following heavy rainfall that flooded the caves. The team, comprising twelve members aged 11 to 16 and their 25-year-old assistant coach, had entered the cave on June 23 after a practice session.

The subsequent rescue operation, one of the most extensive in history, involved approximately 10,000 individuals, including over 100 divers, numerous rescue workers, and representatives from about 100 governmental agencies. The efforts involved mobilizing 900 police officers, 2,000 soldiers, ten police helicopters, seven ambulances, and over 700 diving cylinders. Additionally, more than one billion liters of water were pumped out of the caves to facilitate the rescue.

Following is their incredible true story of survival from one of the most unforgiving environs on earth.

◆

SURVIVING IN A CAVE that is near a source of groundwater always comes with the inherent risk of flooding. Caves, shaped by geological processes, are also often prone to flooding during heavy rainfall or changing weather conditions. The sudden surge of water can transform the subterranean environment into a hazardous situation. Unless a person trapped within a flooded cave can find some high ground, they are sure to drown while being washed away by the current.

Even without the risk of flooding, it's easy to become lost in cave systems. Without any natural light sources, you need to have your own source of light (ideally a flashlight with spare batteries) before entering. Caves can also be icy, but starting a fire in a cave for warmth can be hazardous because if the rock ceiling above you becomes too hot, there is a grave risk of the rock cracking and then crashing over you. Additionally, finding food inside a cave system is nearly impossible, so you would be dependent on whatever food you brought with you inside.

———————◆———————

BENEATH THE CLOUD-SWATHED MOUNTAIN range that separates Thailand and Myanmar (formerly Burma) lies Tham Luang, the fourth-largest cave system in Thailand. Named Tham Luang Khun Nam Nang Non, which translates to "the great cave and water source of the sleeping lady mountain," the cave system extends for over six miles (10 km).

Rich in folklore, Tham Luang is a renowned destination for day-trippers and adventurous children who explore its nooks and crannies. In the rural village of Mae Sai, the cave is a familiar and favorite destination.

Despite its popularity, Tham Luang is not without dangers. The cave system has seen people going missing, contributing to its mystique. As the monsoon season begins in July, the cavern transforms drastically, turning from seemingly innocuous to extremely perilous. During this season, Tham Luang can flood up to 16 feet, making it unsafe for exploration. For safety reasons, authorities generally recommend entering the cave only between November and April.

The epic survival stories in Tham Luang all began with a birthday celebration.

On Saturday, June 23, Peerapat "Night" Sompiangjai turned 17, a momentous occasion typically celebrated with joy. In his rural village in Mae Sai district, Night's family had prepared a vibrant birthday cake and wrapped presents.

However, instead of rushing home, Night, his youth football team friends, and their assistant coach, Ekkapol "Ake" Chantawong, all ventured into the forested hills near the Tham Luang cave. The cave, a favorite exploration spot for the boys, became the unexpected setting for an extraordinarily challenging journey.

Upon reaching the entrance of Tham Luang, they discreetly left their bikes and bags. The team and their young coach were no strangers to the depths of Tham Luang, having explored several miles during initiation rites where they inscribed the names of new team members on a cave wall.

They entered the cave with high spirits, equipped only with their torches, anticipating a brief one or two-hour adventure. Little did they know that their post-practice exploration would soon extend into a two-week struggle for their very lives known around the world. Concerns mounted back at Night's home, where his untouched birthday cake and presents proved unsettling for his family.

———— ◆ ————

INSIDE THE THAM LUANG cave system, the Wild Boars youth football team encountered a dire situation. Persistent rainfall in the preceding days had saturated the mountain, and the water needed an outlet, which was the cave system itself. As rainwater rapidly filled the cave, the boys and their coach faced a flash flood, which caught them off-guard and unprepared.

With the cave system rapidly flooding, the team had no choice but to navigate deeper into the cave to escape the rising waters. Stranded on a small rocky shelf approximately two and a half miles from the entrance, the group found themselves beyond a typically dry point known as Pattaya Beach, which was now fully submerged.

Marooned in the cave's depths, surrounded by darkness, and swallowed by the mountain, the Wild Boars lost all sense of time. Fear and terror invaded their minds. However, their determination to survive prevailed and would eventually carry them through their upcoming ordeal. Utilizing rocks, they dug 15 feet deeper into the shelf, creating a makeshift depression where they could huddle together for warmth. In the face of such adversity, the boys and their coach exhibited remarkable resilience and resourcefulness.

Meanwhile, that evening back at the school, Nopparat Kanthawong, the head coach and founder of the Wild Boars youth football team, checked his phone and discovered over 20 missed calls from anxious parents who hadn't seen their children return. Concerned, Nopparat attempted to contact Ake and several of the boys, but his efforts were unfortunately unsuccessful.

In a pivotal moment, he connected with Songpon Kanthawong, a 13-year-old team member who had separated from the group after practice. Young Songpon informed Coach Nopparat that the other boys had entered the Tham Luang caves.

Responding swiftly to the unfolding situation, Coach Nopparat rushed to the caves and, upon arrival, observed abandoned bicycles and bags near the entrance. Water seeped out of the muddy pathway, indicating a very concerning issue. Recognizing the gravity of the situation, he promptly alerted the authorities to the missing group. Coach Nopparat's timely actions initiated the search and rescue efforts that would soon captivate the world.

Despite the apparent absence of food, the Wild Boars were fortunate to have a source of drinkable water in the form of moisture dripping from the cave walls. While darkness enveloped them, the boys and their coach were equipped with torches for illumination. The porous limestone and rock cracks allowed sufficient oxygen to enter and circulate, providing a fundamental element of life.

Although their situation was far from ideal, the Wild Boars had the essential conditions to endure, at least temporarily. The strength of their unity became a beacon of hope in the face of the unknown. The hardest part of their ordeal lay ahead — their desperate anticipation of rescue. Outside the cave, a comprehensive rescue operation was rapidly forming.

———◆———

BRITISH CAVER VERN UNSWORTH, residing in Chiang Rai and possessing extensive knowledge of the cave complex, had planned a solo expedition for June 24, the day after the team had entered. However, upon receiving news of the missing boys, he advised the Thai government to seek assistance from the British Cave Rescue Council (BCRC). Thai Navy SEALs divers initiated the search on June 25, facing the obstacle of murky water that hindered visibility even with lights. Continuous rain exacerbated the flooding, temporarily halting the search.

On June 27, three BCRC cave divers arrived with specialized equipment, including HeyPhone radios specially designed for cave communications, followed by additional teams of open water divers. A United States Air Force team, reportedly comprising Pararescuemen from the 320th Special Tactics Squadron, the 31st Rescue Squadron, and the 353rd Special Operations Group, joined on June 28. By June 29, an Australian Federal Police team of Specialist Response Group divers had arrived, followed by a Chinese team from the Beijing Peaceland Foundation on July 1.

Simultaneously, surface searches involved policemen with sniffer dogs seeking alternative entrances to the cave system, while drones and robots were deployed for exploration. However, no technology existed to scan for individuals deep underground. The collaborative international effort began a complex and challenging rescue mission.

A logistics camp was established near the cave's entrance, serving as a hub for the extensive rescue operation. The camp accommodated hundreds of volunteers, journalists, and rescue workers, organized into distinct zones. Restricted areas were designated for the Thai Navy SEALs, military personnel, and civilian rescuers, ensuring efficient coordination. A separate zone provided privacy for relatives, while areas for the press and the general public were also delineated.

———◆———

THE RESCUE EFFORT WAS massive, with approximately 10,000 contributors between divers, government agencies, police officers, soldiers, and volunteers. At any given time, more than 500 cylinders were inside the cave, with an additional 200 in the queue for refilling. Remarkably, over a billion liters of water, equivalent to 400 Olympic-sized swimming pools, were successfully pumped out during the operation.

BCRC divers Richard Stanton and John Volanthen, supported by Belgian cave diver Ben Reymenants and French diver Maksym Polejaka, advanced through the cave complex, placing diving guide ropes. The search faced weather-related interruptions, with rainfall increasing water flow, taxing divers with strong currents, and poor visibility. After a necessary hiatus, the search resumed on July 2.

John Volanthen and Rick Stanton navigated the narrow, murky corridors for several days, laying out guide ropes hoping for a breakthrough. Their persistence led them to Pattaya Beach on Monday, but the anticipated signs of life were absent. Undeterred, they pressed forward into the abyss, discovering a crucial air pocket a few hundred meters further in.

Conducting their standard procedure of surfacing, shouting, and sniffing for air spaces, John's torch revealed an awe-inspiring sight: the boys emerging from the darkness toward them. In disbelief, Rick counted the boys while John asked, "How many of you?"

The reply, "Thirteen!" in English, echoed through the cave. Rick, astonished, exclaimed, "They're all alive!"

The two divers, aiming to bolster the boys' morale, spent valuable moments with them before leaving lights and promising to return with food.

A video of the encounter, showcasing the boys' interactions with the divers, was posted on Facebook by the Thai Navy SEALs. Former Chiang Rai provincial governor Narongsak Osatanakorn, who was in charge of the rescue work, announced the discovery, emphasizing that the operation was ongoing.

This alleviated the deep concerns of the Wild Boars' parents, who, after a week of anguish, were overjoyed to witness their children's miraculous survival. The discovery marked a crucial turning point in the rescue mission, setting the stage for the tricky extraction of the trapped students.

———◆———

THE THAI, US, AUSTRALIAN, and Chinese diving teams, supported by BCRC divers, transported diving bottles into the cave system and established an air supply storage area in Chamber 3.

On July 3, three Thai Navy SEALs, including Thai Army doctor Lt. Col. Pak Loharachun, joined the trapped group and provided support until their rescue. Health checks, treatment, and entertainment were offered, and officials reported that none of those trapped were in serious condition.

The Thai Navy's head of Special Forces, Rear Admiral Apagorn Youkonggaew, mentioned that the boys had been fed easy-to-digest, high-energy food with vitamins and minerals under the supervision of a doctor.

A video later released by the Thai Navy SEALs featured all twelve boys and their coach introducing themselves. They were wrapped in emergency blankets and appeared frail but in relatively good spirits. A second video showed a medic treating them.

The trapped group, unable to swim, faced additional challenges in the complex rescue mission. The Army doctor discovered that they had attempted to dig their way out of the cave, using rock fragments to create a hole 16 feet (five meters) deep. To connect with their families, BCRC diver Jason Mallinson offered the boys and Ake an opportunity to send messages using his waterproof notepad. Many notes reassured family members, expressing love, reassurance, and encouragement. This communication played another key role in maintaining the morale of the trapped boys and their families during the harrowing ordeal.

⸻ ◆ ⸻

THE POINT WHERE THE boys and their coach became stranded was approximately two and a half miles from the cave entrance, nestled 3,000 feet below the mountain's summit. The perilous route to reach them presented numerous obstacles, including flooded sections with strong currents, zero visibility, and extremely narrow passages.

The arduous journey into the cave to reach the stranded group required six hours against the current and five hours to exit with the current, a demanding feat even for seasoned divers. The harsh conditions highlighted the complexity of the rescue mission.

From the outset, rescuers grappled with rising water levels. As mitigation, a stone diversion dam was constructed upstream, and pumping systems were installed to extract water from the cave while redirecting inflows. By July 4, pumps were estimated to be removing over 400,000 gallons of water per hour from the cave, albeit causing unintended consequences such as inundating nearby farm fields. Volunteers, in their well-intentioned efforts, inadvertently contributed to the groundwater supply.

Benefiting from a brief period of unseasonably dry weather, these measures led to a reduction in water levels on July 5. The descending levels allowed rescue teams to advance another mile into the cave. However, the looming threat of heavy rains forecasted for that week posed the risk of reversing this progress and potentially flooding the location where the team was trapped, underscoring the ongoing urgency felt by rescuers.

Also, on July 5, tragedy struck as Saman Kunan, a 37-year-old former Thai Navy SEAL and a crucial member of the rescue team, lost his life during a selfless dive. Kunan, who left the SEALs in 2006 and worked in security at Suvarnabhumi Airport, had volunteered for the perilous cave rescue mission.

While delivering air tanks from Chamber 3 to the T-junction near Pattaya Beach, he lost consciousness during his return. Despite attempts at CPR, Kunan could not be revived and was pronounced dead around 1 a.m. on the following day. A member of Thai Navy SEAL Class 30, Kunan's dedication led to his posthumous promotion to lieutenant commander, a seven-rank rise.

Tragically, Beirut Pakbara, another heroic rescue diver and Thai Navy SEAL would succumb to septic shock the following year, resulting from an unspecified latent blood infection he had contracted during the Tham Luang rescue mission.

———————◆———————

ON JULY 6, CONCERNS escalated as the oxygen level inside the cave dropped, heightening fears that the boys might face hypoxia if they remained trapped for an extended period. By July 8, the measured oxygen level had dwindled to 15%, well below the optimal range needed to sustain normal human function, which is around 20%.

In response, Thai military engineers endeavored to install an air supply line for the boys, but this initiative was deemed impractical and subsequently abandoned. The diminishing oxygen levels added urgency to the rescue mission, intensifying the challenges faced by the trapped group and the ongoing efforts to extract them from the cave.

As the crisis unfolded, rescuers devised several strategies to save the trapped team and coach, considering various options to navigate the formidable conditions. The principal approaches included:

- Waiting until the end of the monsoon season. This involved sustaining the team with divers providing necessary supplies like food and water until weather conditions improved.

- Finding an alternative entrance. In the search for alternative entrances that would potentially offer a more accessible route for escape, a shaft that descended 3,000 feet was discovered.

- Drilling a rescue shaft. Over 100 shafts were drilled into the soft limestone to create a passage for extraction, but none proved suitable.

- Building an oxygen line. Establishing a system to deliver additional oxygen to the trapped individuals would address concerns about decreasing oxygen levels.

- Building a telephone wire. By implementing a communication system by installing a telephone wire, they could facilitate contact with the trapped group.

Each option presented its own challenges, and the rescue teams worked tirelessly to evaluate and implement the most viable solution amid the complex and dynamic conditions within the cave system.

Faced with multiple imminent dangers, such as the persistent threat of heavy rainfall, diminishing oxygen levels, and the difficulties of finding or drilling a viable escape passage, rescuers made the critical decision to employ a daring extraction plan.

Initially, there were considerations of teaching the boys basic diving skills, leading to constructing a mock passage for training. However, the final plan evolved to utilize teams of skilled divers to safely navigate the tricky conditions and bring the weakened boys to safety.

The final intricate plan involved experienced divers bringing out the team and coach from the treacherous cave system. The approval of this plan came after consultations between the Thai Navy SEALs, US Air Force rescue experts, and the Thai Minister of the Interior, recognizing the urgency of the situation. 100 divers from Thailand and various countries each played crucial roles. The collaboration between the numerous experts ensured the meticulous refinement of the extraction strategy.

ON THE MORNING OF July 8, officials instructed the media and non-essential personnel to vacate the area around the cave entrance in anticipation of an imminent rescue operation. The looming threat of monsoon rains, expected to persist until October and potentially flood the cave, prompted decisive action.

The extraction process commenced with an assembly of 18 rescue divers, venturing into the caves to extract the boys. A dedicated diver accompanied each boy during their perilous journey out. Leading the international cave diving team were four British divers — John Volanthen, Richard Stanton, Jason Mallinson, and Chris Jewell. Additionally, two Australians, Richard Harris, an anesthesiologist, and Craig Challen, a veterinarian, played crucial roles in the rescue effort.

On the final day of the rescue, Irishman Jim Warny assumed the role of an additional lead diver to bring back assistant coach Ekkapol. The lead divers navigated a challenging route of submerged passages over two miles. Throughout the journey, they were supported by a team of 90 Thai and foreign divers stationed at various points, performing medical check-ups, resupplying air tanks, and executing other emergency roles. These coordinated efforts marked a critical phase in the mission to bring the stranded individuals to safety.

Contrary to conflicting reports regarding the order of rescuing the boys — weakest or strongest first — the actual decision was based on volunteerism. According to Ake, "I talked with Dr. Harris. Everyone was strong and no one was sick...Everybody had a strong mental state. Dr. Harris said... there's no preference."

The group collectively decided that the boys residing the farthest from the cave should be the first to leave. In their July 18 press conference, Ake elaborated on their rationale, stating, "We were thinking, when we get out of the cave, we would have to ride the bicycle home... so the persons who live the furthest away would be allowed to go out first... so that they can go out and tell everyone that we were inside, we were okay."

———— ◆ ————

FOR THE PERILOUS JOURNEY, the boys were outfitted with wetsuits, buoyancy jackets, harnesses, and positive-pressure full-face masks. Before embarking on the rescue, Dr. Harris administered the anesthetic Ketamine to induce a state of complete unconsciousness, a precautionary measure to prevent panic during the journey. This was deemed essential to safeguard both the boys and their rescuers. Additionally, they were given the anti-anxiety drug Alprazolam and the drug atropine to stabilize heart rates and reduce saliva production, minimizing the risk of choking during the hours-long haul out.

Each boy carried a cylinder with 80% oxygen attached to the front and a handle on their back while being tethered to a diver to prevent any loss in the poor visibility conditions. Described by the rescue divers as "a package," they meticulously prepared the boys for this intricate and delicate rescue phase. The Thai government provided Dr. Harris and two medical assistants with diplomatic immunity, offering legal protection in case of unforeseen complications during the rescue operation.

The effects of the initial anesthetic lasted 45 minutes to an hour, necessitating "top-up" ketamine injections administered by divers throughout the three-hour journey. The divers carefully guided the boys through the cave. Depending on the guidelines and in narrow sections, divers gently pushed the boys from behind to navigate through tight passages without dislodging their face masks against rocks. Maintaining a strategic position higher than the boys' heads, divers aimed to absorb potential impacts with rocks first in conditions of poor visibility. The divers were attuned to the boys' breathing through the exhaust bubbles, both visible and palpable.

Upon reaching a dry section following a brief dive, the boys and divers encountered three additional divers. Here, the boys' dive gear was removed, and they were transported on a drag stretcher across an unforgiving terrain of rocks and sand hills spanning over 660 feet (200 meters). Craig Challen assessed their conditions, and the boys' dive gear was reinstated before they were again submerged for the ensuing section. The boys arrived at 45-minute intervals, ensuring a careful and staged progression through the intricate rescue parade.

When they reached the staging base in Chamber 3, the boys were seamlessly passed along a "daisy chain" orchestrated by hundreds of rescuers stationed along the precarious path out of the cave. Wrapped in Sked stretchers, they were alternately carried, slid, and zip-lined over a complex network of pulleys set up by rock climbers. The complicated terrain, partially submerged in many areas from Chamber 3 to the cave entrance, required rescuers to transport the boys over slippery rocks and through muddy water for hours.

———— ♦ ————

ONGOING EFFORTS TO DRAIN and clear the mud path using shovels steadily reduced the extraction time to two hours after a week of dedicated work. Authorities cautioned that the extraction process would span several days, as crews needed to replace air tanks, gear, and other supplies, necessitating 10-20 hours between each run. Shortly after 7:00 p.m., local officials confirmed that two boys had been rescued and transported to Chiangrai Prachanukroh Hospital. Subsequently, two more boys exited the cave and underwent assessments by medical officials. The expedited rescues were attributed to lower water levels resulting from improved weather conditions and constructing a weir outside the cave to manage water flow.

On July 9, the successful rescue operation continued as four more boys were safely extracted from the cave. The following day, the final four boys, along with their assistant coach, were successfully rescued, marking the conclusion of the intricate and challenging mission. Throughout the rescue operation, the collective experience and refined procedures contributed to streamlining the extraction process. The time required to extract each boy decreased daily, enabling the efficient rescue of the last four boys and their coach on the final day.

The three Thai Navy SEALs and the Army doctor, who had dedicatedly stayed with the boys throughout the ordeal, were the last to embark on the treacherous dive to safety. Unfortunately, as they made their way to Chamber 3 where rescuers were stationed, an unforeseen issue arose when the pumps shut off, potentially due to a burst water pipe. The sudden halt in pumping operations led to rising water levels in Chamber 3, which posed a significant risk of cutting off access to Chamber 2, Chamber 1, and the cave entrance.

Faced with this unexpected challenge, up to 100 rescuers, still positioned more than 1.5 kilometers inside the cave, had to evacuate rapidly, leaving behind essential rescue equipment. The urgency of the situation required them to navigate the cave exit swiftly, with the last diver making it back to Chamber 3 just as everyone was preparing to leave.

———————◆———————

THE SUCCESSFUL EXTRACTION OF the Thai cave boys and Coach Ake was an extraordinary accomplishment, bringing an end to two weeks of intense anticipation and concern.

Throughout Chiang Rai province, the atmosphere was jubilation. Ecstatic crowds lined the streets leading to the hospital, cheering on the ambulances transporting the rescued individuals. The celebratory sounds of blaring car horns resonated through the air, adding to the festive spirit. Thai social media platforms were flooded with posts carrying hashtags such as #ThankYou, #Heroes, and #Hooyah—the distinctive Thai Navy Seal chant.

Across the globe, millions of people who had anxiously followed the unfolding story celebrated the safe return of the Wild Boars. The collective relief and joy echoed the shared humanity that transcended borders, emphasizing the power of unity and compassion in the face of adversity.

In their hospital beds, wearing gowns and face masks, the Thai cave boys made a public appearance, sitting up and waving to the world. A video released by the Thai Navy Seals on July 11 provided the media with the first post-rescue glimpse of the Wild Boars, with some of the boys flashing victory signs at the camera.

Unfortunately, their parents, who had anxiously awaited their sons' returns, were not physically present in the room; instead, they observed the heartwarming scene through a viewing window, overcome with joy and, sometimes, tears.

The Thai government justified quarantining the boys to safeguard their health and prevent potential infections. Prime Minister Prayuth Chan-ocha personally visited the boys, emphasizing the seriousness of the situation.

Despite the strict rules, the parents did not publicly object. The boys reportedly consumed rice porridge, with more complex foods withheld for ten days. According to the Thai Health Ministry, the boys were in "good condition," though having lost an average of 4.4 pounds (2 kg) each. They were expected to remain hospitalized for at least a week.

Stringent precautions were taken during the initial visits, with parents observing through windows. If subsequent laboratory results proved pessimistic, they would be permitted to visit in person, wearing medical gowns, face masks, and hair caps.

To ensure the well-being of the boys, detailed tests on their eyes, nutrition, mental health, and blood were conducted. A Health Ministry physician noted increased white blood cells in all the boys, prompting preventive antibiotic doses for the entire team. The boys, taking precautions, wore sunglasses to aid their eyes in adjusting to daylight.

Plans were announced to transform the cave system into a living museum, showcasing the remarkable operation that saved the Wild Boars. In response to the incident, Thailand's Navy SEALs decided to incorporate cave-diving into their training regimen, aiming to enhance their preparedness for any similar emergencies in the future.

Highlighting a unique aspect of the rescued individuals, three boys and their assistant coach were stateless, meaning they held no citizenship in any country. Officials committed to grant them Thai citizenship within six months, a promise fulfilled on September 26 when the four individuals were officially granted Thai citizenship.

The incredible story of the rescue of the twelve Thai boys and Ake, their assistant coach, will be forever remembered. In 2022, the incident was retold in the motion picture *Thirteen Lives*, directed by Ron Howard.

Conclusion

What can we learn and apply to our own lives?

EACH OF THESE ASTONISHING survival accounts is ripe with learning opportunities. Let's review some of the essential survival lessons we can glean from these stories and consider which skill sets we could develop more robustly to increase our knowledge and chances of survival should we ever be confronted with similar life-or-death scenarios.

Essential Survival Skills

From the stores herein, we can glean the following eight categories of survival preparedness and emergency coping lessons.

Survival Skill Set #1: Mental Resilience and Positive Mindset

- Maintaining mental resilience and a positive mindset is often overlooked, yet it is vital for survival. Enduring harsh conditions and overcoming psychological challenges are integral. Juliane Koepcke's ability to endure the harrowing experience in the Amazon jungle demonstrates the importance of mental resilience.

- Similarly, Zamperini also displayed incredible mental resilience to survive a plane crash and the rest of the war as a POW. As did James Riley and his crew members when they were captured in the Sahara Desert, and Joe Simpson who resolutely forged his way through what could have been his ice dungeon and grave.

Survival Skill Set #2: Problem Solving and Decision Making

- Effective problem-solving and decision-making skills are crucial for survival. This involves quickly assessing a situation, identifying potential threats, and making informed decisions under pressure. An exemplary model of strength of mind is that of Shackleton, whose entire ship crew survived under his decisive servant-leadership.

Survival Skill Set #3: Resourcefulness and Adaptability

- Survivors often exhibit resourcefulness and adaptability in bleak situations. This involves the ability to assess available resources, think creatively, and adapt plans based on ever-changing conditions. As an excellent example, while being adrift at sea for over a year, Alvagrenga had to adapt to the environment, utilize available resources, and creatively find ways to sustain himself.

- Likewise Riley and Zamperini, in their unique circumstances, never gave up on 'working the problem' at hand to find their way through the dark maze and back into the light of freedom.

Survival Skill Set #4: Wilderness Orientation and Navigation

- Navigating through unfamiliar and challenging terrain is a crucial survival skill. This includes map reading, using a compass, recognizing natural landmarks, and understanding the basics of navigation. As stellar examples, the collective navigation skills of the Thai cave rescue team saved 13 young lives. Likewise, Koepcke's survival in the Amazon jungle involved navigating through dense vegetation and following water sources like her father had taught her, showcasing the importance of wilderness navigation in finding safety.

- Orientational skills are also vital for understanding one's surroundings, avoiding getting lost, and finding a way to safety. This includes using natural markers, reading maps, and utilizing navigation tools. Developing direction-finding skills and understanding basic navigation techniques can be life-saving in various survival scenarios. Among a collection of survival skills, Shackleton's ability to read maps and use a sextant saved his and his crew's lives.

Survival Skill Set #5: Fire Building and Shelter Construction

- The ability to build a fire and create shelter is fundamental for staying warm, dry, and protected in various environments. This skill is especially crucial in harsh weather conditions. Angela Hernandez, trapped on a rocky beach, might have benefited from fire-building and shelter-construction skills to enhance her chances of staying warm and signaling for help. These skills contribute to maintaining core body temperature and providing a sense of security in the wild.

- For instance, Shackleton and his crew used the lifeboats to create makeshift shelters after they were forced to evacuate the *Endurance*. This, in addition to getting a fire going, is no doubt what allowed them to survive in the freezing Antarctic environment.

Survival Skill #6: Food and Water Procurement

- Knowing how to procure food and water from the wild is a vital survival skill. This includes identifying edible plants, catching fish, trapping animals, and foraging for food. Had Riley and his crew been able to source clean water and nutritional sustenance during their captivity in the Sahara, their physical and mental health would have fared much better.

- The Robertson family's experience highlights the importance of adapting to the available resources at sea, where they hunted turtles and fish to sustain themselves and used turtle blood as an alternative to water to stay hydrated. We also saw this with Alvarenga as he used his skills as a fisherman to fish for sharks and fish and even waited to grab birds that landed on his boat so he could eat them as well.

Survival Skill Set #7: First Aid and Medical Knowledge

- Basic first-aid skills and medical knowledge are essential for treating injuries and illnesses in survival situations. The Robertson family's experience at sea underscores the importance of understanding basic medical procedures, as they had to address injuries, cope with dehydration, and improvise medical solutions during their extended ordeal.

- First-aid knowledge can be a life-saving skill when professional medical help is unavailable. Juliane Kopecke's efforts to treat her wounds, which were becoming infested with maggots, showcase this importance. When trained medical personnel are available, as with the Thai cave rescue team, the danger to health and life can be significantly reduced.

Survival Skill Set #8: Signaling and Communication

- Signaling for help and communicating with potential rescuers is essential in survival scenarios. This includes knowing distress signals, using signaling devices, and improvising communication methods. Effective signaling techniques might have reduced the length of Angela Hernandez's suffering on the rocky beach, as would Simpson's and Zamperini's. Mastering signaling and communication enhances the chances of being noticed and rescued in remote locations.

Each of the above skill groups is equally important for getting us through a survival situation. But if there is one internal characteristic resounding within each person in these stories, it is their mental resilience, unwavering determination, and indomitable spirit to survive and thrive.

———— ◆ ————

Sharpening Your Tools

EACH PERSON IN OUR survival accounts, from Captain Riley imagining his reunion with his family to Alvarenga imagining a better life once he was found, was able to use hope as their tool of resilience.

In the face of great adversity, hope can serve as the cornerstone, allowing individuals to shift their focus from overwhelming obstacles to actionable steps within their control. This optimistic outlook not only boosts morale but also fosters a sense of empowerment, encouraging proactive responses.

Adaptability is another key component of mental resilience. Survival often demands quick adjustments to ever-changing circumstances. Those who can adapt effectively are better equipped to overcome unforeseen challenges, turning potential setbacks into opportunities for growth. This flexibility allows individuals to embrace change and navigate uncertainties with greater ease.

Managing stress is critical to maintaining mental resilience. Stress-reduction techniques, such as deep breathing exercises and mindfulness practices, help regulate emotional responses. By staying grounded and composed, individuals can approach problems with a clear mind, enhancing their decision-making capabilities even in high-pressure situations.

Self-care is equally important in sustaining mental well-being during survival scenarios. Prioritizing physical health, adequate rest, and nutrition ensures that individuals are better equipped to face their environment's demands. Establishing a routine with these elements contributes to overall mental and physical resilience.

Goal setting is a strategic approach to survival, breaking down overarching objectives into manageable tasks. This systematic approach provides direction and a sense of purpose, enabling individuals to make progress in even the most arduous of circumstances. Resilient problem-solving goes hand in hand with adaptability, emphasizing the ability to learn from experiences and adjust strategies accordingly.

Social connections act as powerful morale boosters. In survival situations, collaboration and shared responsibilities among a group contribute to a collective sense of support. We saw this strongly amongst Captain Riley and his men, as well as Shackleton and his crew. This camaraderie not only provides emotional sustenance but also increases the likelihood of finding innovative solutions to problems.

Learning from life-threatening experiences is an ongoing process that refines one's mental toolkit. Each survival situation offers lessons that can be applied to future scenarios, enhancing preparedness and adaptive capabilities.

Amazing Hunting Survival Stories

To GAIN ADDITIONAL INSPIRATION and survival knowledge, many readers have found my book *Amazing Hunting Survival Stories: Wilderness Adventure Tales that Teach Practical Skills & Inspire Extraordinary Perseverance* to be an excellent companion to this book.

Amazing Hunting Survival Stories is a captivating compilation of fictional yet true-to-life tales about hunters who overcame life-threatening wild animal encounters by promptly taking effective action coupled with incredible resilience.

In your wildest imagination, have you ever wondered if – and how – you could survive life-threatening hunting scenarios?

• While going deer hunting alone in the Oregon Cascades, **your canoe capsizes, resulting in a concussion**.

• During your hike in the Idaho Rockies to hunt elk, **you and your daughter get stranded by a blizzard**.

• As you trek the tundra to join your moose hunting party in the Brooks Range of Alaska, **a Grizzly Bear mauls you**.

• While hiking the Mojave Desert in Utah to hunt Pronghorn, **you are bitten by a rattlesnake**.

• As you and your archery buddy row through the Florida Everglades to hunt wild hogs, **your old boat capsizes in the alligator-inhabited swamp**.

• As young newlyweds hunting whitetail deer in the Kentucky Appalachians, you follow a prized buck into a cave – only to get lost in the subterranean darkness; **a cave-in further hinders you**.

If you were in their hiking boots, would you have the resilience to regulate your intense emotions and take reason-based actions to return to your loved ones unscathed?

Come inside to vicariously face their challenges, **test your survival knowledge** required to escape these hunting scenarios, and learn how our characters survived their harrowing ordeals.

Dive in and start reading right now. These **thrilling stories** will transport you right into the midst of the adventure, igniting your imagination.

Phoenix MacLeod books

Your Next Steps

So what's next for you?

Simple: to fundamentally realize that you are a lot stronger and more capable than you ever considered yourself to be.

I hope these compelling survival stories inspire you to prepare by illuminating the indomitable human spirit in the face of adversity. They stand as vivid reminders of the remarkable strength each individual holds within, demonstrating that even in the most harrowing circumstances, the human will to survive can prevail against seemingly insurmountable odds.

Whether you ever find yourself in a survival situation or not, you want to be ready. Each person in these stories possessed unique skills that they used to aid in their survival. Alveranga used his skills as a fisherman to sustain himself for over a year at sea. Juliane Kopecke used her knowledge of the jungle from her personal experiences to get out.

All the same, you'll want to learn more about survival. You can possess at least some experience before you find yourself trapped in the wild. That's why I'd start by learning first aid in a wilderness first aid course, spending time starting campfires, and building shelters in the woods. Then you can keep building your skills from there.

These stories are not just about survival; they are about resilience, resourcefulness, and the unwavering determination to navigate life's most challenging obstacles successfully. They depict individuals who, when confronted with the harshest of conditions, summoned an extraordinary inner strength to defy fate and emerge alive.

In closing, may the stories herein inspire you and remind you of the strength each of us holds within. May they motivate you to face life's challenges with courage, resourcefulness, and an unwavering will to prevail.

Joyfully,
Phoenix MacLeod
Survival Wisdom from an Off-Grid Survivor
https://www.phoenixmacleod.com/

P.S. For anyone who is currently doubting their own perseverance: No matter how tough life may seem right now, how heavy your burdens may weigh, or how alone you may feel, please hear me and believe:

Your unique and valuable story is NEVER OVER – as long as you NEVER GIVE UP – and DO NOT LOSE HOPE!
For you are indeed known and loved.

The steadfast love of the Lord never ceases; his mercies never come to an end; they are new every morning; great is your faithfulness.
- Lamentations 3:22-23 (ESV)

Please Help Other Readers

Do you know why the Dead Sea is 'dead'? It cannot sustain life because it only receives (water) and does not give back. So, it remains salty, stale, and stagnant.

We've each been blessed to be a blessing to others. Now is your chance to make a positive difference in the lives of families you've never met.

If you have gained knowledge and inspiration from this book, then be blessed by informing others of its benefits. Kindly **invest one minute to share your review.**

Please share a review

https://reviewprojects.phoenixmacleod.com/world

P.S. Thank you for your thoughtful action. Other readers and I genuinely appreciate your input.

Free PDF Booklet for You

Here's a FREE GIFT for your family!

To bring even more value to you, you are welcome to receive this **free PDF of a 50-page booklet with 120 fun and creative outdoor activities** (organized by season).

To **receive your free PDF** and very few emails informing you of my next book of survival prepping projects or incredible survival stories, visit here:

https://www.phoenixmacleod.com/familypdf

References

Chapter 1

- Cavanaugh, Ray. (2016, February 16th). "From Connecticut Captain to African Slave - and Back." *CT-Post. https://www.ctpost.com/opinion/article/From-Connecticut-captain-to-African-slave-and-6834333.php*

- Fenicle, Joseph D. (2017, January 21st). "Captain James Riley - The Sea, The Sahara, the Swamp, and the Sea." *The American Surveyor. https://amerisurv.com/2017/01/21/captain-james-riley-the-sea-the-sahara-the-swamp-and-the-sea/*

- George. (n.d.). "The Story of Resilience - Captain James Riley." *Leaders Principles. https://leadersprinciples.com/the-story-of-resilience-captain-james-riley/*

- Rubin, Martin. (2004, February 22nd). "Into the Fire - A Captain and his Crew Survive a Shipwreck Only To Become Slaves in the African Desert." *SF-Gate. https://www.sfgate.com/books/article/into-the-fire-a-captain-and-his-crew-survive-a-2820423.php*

- Unknown Author. (n.d.). "Captain James Riley." *Bushcraft*

Buddy. https://bushcraftbuddy.com/captain-james-riley-strand
ed-and-enslaved/

Chapter 2

- Breese, Amber. (2023, July 3rd). "The Doomed Journey of the Endurance Ship and Her Miraculous Discovery Over a Century Later." *All That's Interesting.* https://allthatsinteresting.com/en durance-ship

- Unknown Author. (n.d.). "History of Endurance." *Endurance22.* https://endurance22.org/history-of-endurance

- Unknown Author. (n.d.). "Ernest Shackleton." *Wikipedia.* h ttps://en.wikipedia.org/wiki/Ernest_Shackleton

Chapter 3

- Cabral, Carrie. (2020, August 17th). "How Louis Zamperini's POW Days Shaped His Life." *Shortform.* https://www.shortfor m.com/blog/louis-zamperini-pow/

- Green, Richard. (2014, December 24th). "Louis Zamperini: The Story of a True American Hero." *Unwritten Records.* https://unwritten-record.blogs.archives.gov/2014/12/2 4/louis-zamperini-the-story-of-a-true-american-hero/

- Associated Press. (2014, July 3rd). "Louis Zamperini, World War II hero and Olympian, dies." *USA Today.* https://www.usatoday.com/story/sports/olympics/2014/07/03/lou is-zamperini-olympic-runner-world-war-ii-veteran-dies/121326 99/

- Piette, Lauren. (n.d.). "Faith and Forgiveness: The Rest of Louis Zamperini's Story." *Veteran Life.* https://veteranlife.com/lifesty

le/louis-zamperini/

- Unknown Author. (2020, October 2nd). "Louis Zamperini." *Biography. https://www.biography.com/military-figures/louis-zamperini*

- Unknown Author. (2021, June 17th). "Great Survival Stories: Louis Zamperini." *Explorers Web. https://explorersweb.com/great-survival-stories-louis-zamperini/*

Chapter 4

- Armitage, Rebecca. (2022, October). "How Teenager Juliane Koepcke Survived A Plane Crash and Solo 11 Day Trek Out of the Amazon." *ABC News. https://www.abc.net.au/news/2022-10-02/the-girl-who-fell-3km-into-the-amazon-and-survived/101413154*

- Goldfarb, Kara. (2023, November 1st). "The Incredible Story Of Juliane Koepcke, The Teenager Who Fell 10,000 Feet Out Of A Plane And Somehow Survived." *All That's Interesting. https://allthatsinteresting.com/juliane-koepcke*

- Koepcke, Julia. (2012, March 24th). "How I Survived A Plane Crash." *BBC. https://www.bbc.com/news/magazine-17476615*

- Taylor, Jessica. (2023, June 12th). "How girl, 17, survived 11 days alone in the Amazon Rainforest after a plane crash in 1971: Juliane Koepcke swam piranha-occupied waters and tended to wounds infested with maggots before being rescued." *Daily Mail. How-Juliane-Koepcke-17-survived-11-days-Amazon-Rainforest-plane-crash.html*

Chapter 5

- Unknown Author. (2012, July 18th). "Shipwrecked By Whales: The Robertson Family Survival Story." *BBC. https://www.bbc. com/news/uk-england-stoke-staffordshire-18877090*

- Unknown Author. (2021, February 20th). "Great Survival Stories: The Robertson Family." *Explorers Web. https://explorersw eb.com/great-survival-stories-the-robertson-family/*

- Williams, Sally. (2009, August 21st). "Shipwrecked: Nightmare in the Pacific." *The Guardian. https://www.theguardian.com/l ifeandstyle/2009/aug/22/shipwreck-lucette-sailing*

Chapter 6

- Eneix, Neal. (n.d). "Mountain Survival: The True Story of Joe Simpson." *Survivalist Gear. https://survivalistgear.co/mountai n-survival-the-true-story-of-joe-simpson/*

- Gogorza, Oscar. (2021, October 13th). "Touching the Void: Would You Cut the Rope to Survive?" *English El- pais. https://english.elpais.com/usa/2021-10-13/touching-the-voi d-would-you-cut-the-rope-to-survive.html*

- Guise, Tom. (2020, January 14th). "Joe Simpson Recalls One of Mountaineering's Greatest Survival Stories." *Red Bull. https://www.redbull.com/us-en/theredbulletin/joe-simpson -touching-the-void-interview*

- Lewis, Tim. (2019, November 9th). "Joe Simpson: To Be A Serious Climber, You Have To Be A Little BIt Unhinged." *The Guardian. https://www.theguardian.com/books/2019/nov/ 09/joe-simpson-interview-touching-the-void*

- Unknown Author. (n.d.). "Touching the Void." *Wikipedia.* *https://en.wikipedia.org/wiki/Touching_the_Void_(book)*

Chapter 7

- Epstein, David. (2021, April 18th). "How I Survived 438 Days Adrift in the Pacific Ocean." *Slate. https://slate.com/human-interest/2021/04/438-days-lost-at-sea-jose-salvador-alvarenga.html*

- Franklin, Jonathan. (2015, November 7th). "Lost at Sea: The Man Who Vanished For 14 Months." *The Guardian. https://www.theguardian.com/world/2015/nov/07/fisherman-lost-at-sea-436-days-book-extract*

- Serena, Katie. (n.d.). "The Incredible Story of Jose Salvador Alvarenga - Who Survived 438 Days Adrift in the Pacific." *All That's Interesting. https://allthatsinteresting.com/jose-alvarenga*

- Unknown Author. (n.d.). "Jose Salvador Alvarenga." *Wikipedia. https://en.wikipedia.org/wiki/José_Salvador_Alvarenga*

Chapter 8

- Bever, Lindsey. (2018, July 16th). "How a woman swerved off a 200-foot cliff and survived 7 days trapped on a secluded beach." *Washington Post. https://www.washingtonpost.com/news/post-nation/wp/2018/07/16/how-a-woman-swerved-off-a-200-foot-cliff-and-survived-7-days-trapped-on-a-secluded-beach/#:~:text=She%20veered%20off%20the%20edge,water%20rising%20over%20my%20knees.*

- Copitch, Josh. (2019, July 16th). "1 year ago: Woman who survived 7 days on Big Sur beach shares crash photos."

KSBW. *https://www.ksbw.com/article/1-year-ago-woman-who-s urvived-7-days-on-big-sur-beach-shares-crash-photos/28414650*

- Rosenblatt, Kalhan. (2018, July 16th). "Oregon woman survives week on remote beach after plunge off California cliff." *NBC   News. https://www.nbcnews.com/news/us-news/oregon-woman-survives -week-remote-beach-after-plunge-california-cliff-n891646*

Chapter 9

- Paddock, Richard C. and Muktita Suhartono. (2018, July 2nd). "Soccer Team is Found Alive in Thailand Cave Rescue." *The New York Times. https://www.nytimes.com/2018/07/02/world/ asia/thailand-boys-rescued.html*

- Unknown Author. (2018, July 13th). "The Full Story of Thailand's Extraordinary Cave Rescue." *BBC. https://www.bbc.com /news/world-asia-44791998*

Conclusion

- English Standard Version Bible. (2001). Crossway.

Printed in Great Britain
by Amazon

54703866R00076